HELLSTRIP
GARDENING

Hellstrip
GARDENING

**Create a paradise
between the sidewalk
and the curb**

Evelyn J. Hadden

With photographs by Joshua McCullough

Foreword by Lauren Springer Ogden

Frontispiece: Nothing enlivens a cementscape more than a
boldly blooming garden.

Photo and location credits appear on page 282.

The Haseltine Building   6a Lonsdale Road
133 S.W. Second Avenue, Suite 450   London NW6 6RD
Portland, Oregon 97204-3527   timberpress.co.uk
timberpress.com

Printed in China
Book design by Breanna Goodrow

Library of Congress Cataloging-in-Publication Data

Hadden, Evelyn J.
  Hellstrip gardening : create a paradise between the sidewalk
and the curb / Evelyn J. Hadden ; with
photographs by Joshua McCullough ; foreword by Lauren
Springer Ogden. -- 1st ed.
      p. cm.
  Includes bibliographical references and index.
  ISBN 978-1-60469-332-4
  1. Urban gardening--United States. 2. Curbs--United States.
I. Title.
  SB453.H18 2014
  635.09173'2--dc23
                2013040747

Contents

PART ONE

Inspirations
Curbside Gardens from Coast to Coast

PART TWO

Situations
Challenges to Address, Obstacles to Overcome

Foreword

by Lauren Springer Ogden

All garden spaces are not created equal; in fact, some are overlooked as candidates for any gardening at all. This unique book embraces these forlorn spots, giving the reader compelling reasons as well as the tools needed not only to dig in but also to enjoy success creating and stewarding the newly transformed areas.

Just as homeowners and even seasoned gardeners are often intimidated by the idea of annexing such areas, authors have not had the courage, conviction, and optimism to forge ahead and write about this topic. Such writing is long overdue. Evelyn Hadden's intelligence shines throughout this gem of a book. She offers a rare combination of sensitive and thoughtful treatment of the big picture and dogged, thorough coverage of things practical. This makes her thesis—that such small, seemingly meaningless places can change a home, a neighborhood, a community—utterly believable. Her wise and encouraging words give the reader pause and motivate the skeptic among us to consider picking up the shovel.

Hadden then takes the reader by the hand and shows how to do it. No stone is left unturned: we are led head-on through the joys and potential pitfalls. Practical advice on horticultural topics such as soil, water, and plants abounds. This is joined by evenhanded, generous advice on the more unusual situations that these gardens often engender, such as covenants and regulations and how to negotiate them with more positive outcomes. She graciously exhorts the reader to share plants with neighbors, to open curbside gardens to passersby, and to gently push for change in existing ideals and practices that stifle gardens, promoting community rather than rebellion. I wish I had read her advice twenty-five years ago before embarking on my conflict-fraught first hellstrips, where as a zealous young upstart I spent as much time (or more) butting heads with neighbors and town authorities as I did tending and enjoying the new gardens.

As Hadden makes a case for these gardens and teaches us to succeed with them, she is welcoming and positive, yet always matter-of-fact, practical, fair, and not preachy. "Give that leftover a makeover," she cheers, and then gives the reader the dirt on how to do it, literally and figuratively. Her honesty is refreshing,

especially in light of the prevalent misguided claim that lawn alternatives are lower maintenance. Of course a fabulous curbside garden will require more tending than an abandoned plot or even a poorly tended strip of lawn. This book faces down these challenges and doesn't mislead. And what's more, the information and advice given here transcends these difficult spots and can be applied to gardens of all sorts.

Open the pages that follow and begin a journey that can make a difference to you and your neighborhood, that impacts people, plants, animals—the web of life around you. Take part in creating corridors of diversity by adding environmentally intelligent garden snippets to serve as lively sanctuaries in this ever more crowded and unnatural world. With the help of this fine book, stretch your gardening wings and garden space, create curb appeal for bees, birds, butterflies, and passersby alike, and watch dogs stop, sniff, and then continue on down the road to find some lawn or bare patch to do their business. After reading this book, you may wish for more unloved, forlorn spots on which to work some garden magic.

Introduction

Why Curbside Landscapes Matter

Curbside gardens are an essential ingredient of pleasant, walkable neighborhoods.

Many of us own or manage pieces of land that are part of the public landscape, a landscape that other people interact with every day. That public environment uplifts our mood or sends it plummeting, rivets us in the present moment or fails to distract us from our busyness. Attractive scenes invite us to open our senses and our hearts, while ugly or barren surroundings train us to block those sensory messages.

Yes, curbside landscapes have that much power. And by extension, we who own and manage those landscapes also have power.

I invite you to use your power, to make your own contribution to the public landscape. Convert a sparse, weed-ridden curbside lawn to smile-inducing scenery that doesn't need much help to stay healthy. Outside the fence, down the steps, or beside the driveway, incorporate ignored and deplored bits of land into the rest of your garden, or help them shine as stand-alone pocket gardens that brighten the routes of commuters.

You'll add curb appeal, and you'll also improve the daily life of your neighborhood and its denizens. The gifts

of a curbside garden are disproportionately large. Natural scenes, even minutely glimpsed in passing, distract us from worry and interrupt negative psychological cycles. Garden fragments purify and freshen air, absorb and filter water, and foster biodiversity with its associated services and benefits, not to mention lowering crime and raising property values.

With just one garden, you can make living where you live—and visiting too—more fragrant, more lively, more peaceful, more interesting, more earth-friendly, and more appealing.

What Are Curbside Gardens?

Curbside locations are the public faces of places. Though they are the last areas we may think to beautify, they provide the first glimpses of what to expect inside a building, through a gate, or across a threshold. They may be the places most used by wildlife passing through our properties, and the places where runoff, litter, and human visitors are apt to loiter. These tough environments don't often support healthy lawns, but they can host thriving gardens that dramatically improve their surroundings.

Parking strips (the piece of land between a street and a public sidewalk, also known as a tree park, boulevard, verge, hellstrip, meridian, planting strip, or inferno strip) make promising spots for curbside gardens. So do front yards that are simply one outdoor room from curbside to front door. Although the most challenging area of such a front yard may be located alongside the street, driveway, or public walk, the gardener will likely want to design the entire room as a whole, not just one edge of it.

Similar challenges and opportunities exist for fragments of land languishing alongside driveways and buildings and in alleys, parking lots, roundabouts, and medians. Some of these places may be publicly owned or have public easements or utilities running through them, posing additional challenges and perhaps limiting the types of plants and structures that can be added. Regulations are most often set by the city but can vary from neighborhood to neighborhood.

Who's Doing It?

Across North America, gardeners are tackling this final frontier. Curbside gardeners include water savers, edible gardeners, wilderness advocates, busy homeowners, creative thinkers, green-starved urban dwellers, and generous neighbors. Savvy businesses, government agencies, and neighborhood organizations too are realizing the rewards of remaking these landscapes.

Water scarcity and rising costs for irrigation are driving many of the changes. Western regions and those facing water restrictions and long-term droughts have turned their attention to relandscaping medians, boulevards, and parking lot islands, as well as unused turf areas around government and commercial buildings. Climate-appropriate planting reduces or eliminates the

A hedge of hollyhocks (*Alcea rosea*) and Russian sage (*Perovskia atriplicifolia*) encircles a seating area in a Laramie, Wyoming, pocket park.

below In her classic book *The Undaunted Garden*, author and landscape designer Lauren Springer Ogden coined the term *hellstrip* to describe this tough-to-plant area that she transformed along her street.

need to irrigate, while rain gardens collect storm water runoff from expanses of roof and pavement and encourage it to soak into soil and roots, filtering out pollutants and bypassing costly wastewater treatment.

Water authorities often fund these redesigns, which may put off or prevent costly facility upgrades. In neighborhoods that face expensive street or storm sewer upgrades to protect water quality or control runoff, a city may choose a less costly retrofit, cutting curbs, digging rain gardens, and even installing plants for residents who opt in. Where demand for water outstrips the supply, regional water authorities have begun paying residents to convert lawns to less thirsty alternatives.

Individual gardeners and their families can see cost savings from converting unused, unloved, and sometimes unkempt curbside lawns to gardens. Want to cut your home heating and cooling costs? Plant trees and shrubs to block sun and wind; as they grow up, your bills will go down. Does the basement flood? Does ice accumulate on the driveway? Put a garden to work soaking up water before it can damage structures and impair safety. Harder to quantify but key to an enjoyable daily life, intangibles such as privacy and comfort can be directly influenced by curbside landscapes.

Mounting distrust of industrially produced food is also leading many families to swap some lawn for edible gardens. As our favorite common vegetables and fruits prefer sunny places, the front yard and the parking strip have become desirable sites for food gardens. Despite pushback from some communities and regulations that favor lawns over fresh herbs and produce, more curbside vegetable gardens are born every day.

Restaurants with a focus on serving fresh food find it convenient and good for business to grow more of it on-site, which often means streetside in front of their shop. Challenges aside, what better way to entice customers than to show them fresh food before they walk through the door?

Community gardens are multiplying like rabbits. Students are building and tending gardens at school. The city of Seattle began a multi-year joint venture with local volunteer groups to plant a food forest in an urban park. Thanks to First Lady Michelle Obama, the White House lawn sprouted a vegetable garden. Growing healthy food is no longer an afterthought or an activity relegated to

opposite When a 30-plus-acre parking lot in Maplewood, Minnesota, was pinpointed as a major source of urban runoff and phosphorus reaching a nearby creek and lake, the Ramsey-Washington Metro Watershed District retrofitted it with rain gardens, tree trenches, and porous pavement.

An abandoned elevated freight railway in New York City, reclaimed as High Line Park, is home to a diverse mix of tough plants, including many natives.

Side-by-side lawnless front gardens serve up double delight in Boise, Idaho.

the backyard, but a primary pastime, to be enjoyed out in the open and shared with friends, neighbors, and community.

As development claims more open space in urban areas, city planners are moving to protect and even increase urban green spaces. Public parks and gardens bring the experience of nature into our cities, contributing spring greenery, summer flowers, fall foliage, and organic shapes visible throughout the winter against the hard lines of buildings and pavement. Formerly, when wild nature was more common, a lawn with a few trees might be considered a perfectly satisfactory green space. Now, though lawns are useful for a limited range of human activities, they are best balanced with more densely vegetated areas that host wildlife, capture atmospheric carbon, buffer shorelines, and perform an assortment of other services that protect biodiversity as well as the air we breathe and the water we drink.

Entire cities have become curbside-garden friendly. When Saint Paul and Minneapolis revised their boulevard ordinances to allow plants up to 36 inches tall on the strip of land between the sidewalk and the street, boulevard gardens began popping up. Urban gardeners who had filled their properties to their limits could finally expand their territory. Citywide boulevard garden contests and tours were born. Years after the revised ordinances took effect, it is not uncommon to see entire front yards that have become pocket prairies or cottage gardens or urban farms, stretching across the sidewalks to incorporate the parking strips, and even entire city blocks of diverse, lawnless front yards.

As more gardens grow, the ideas and extra plants they generate fuel new gardens and ignite new gardeners. Citywide transformations are under way in Boise, Boulder, Buffalo, Berkeley, Phoenix, Portland, Seattle,

opposite, top left Colorful foliage and flowers hug a public sidewalk in Portland, Oregon, where hellstrip gardens are proliferating.

opposite, center left Mesa, Arizona, is one of a growing list of cities offering financial incentives to residents who replace lawns with more waterwise landscapes.

opposite, bottom left Buffalo, New York, a leader in curbside gardening, attracts tens of thousands of visitors to its annual self-guided tour, Garden Walk Buffalo.

opposite, top right Neighbors worked together to make this San Francisco sidewalk more permeable by retrofitting it with many tiny gardens; similar paving-to-planting conversions are taking place throughout the city.

opposite, bottom right Dry-adapted plantings in downtown Boulder, Colorado, incorporate grasses, trees and shrubs, and decorative annual flowers.

New Orleans, and many, many other metropolitan areas, where urban gardeners are steadily converting unused streetside lawns to landscapes that support healthy street trees, pollinator-friendly flowers, ornamental grasses, and fruits, vegetables, and herbs.

Rewards of Curbside Gardening

Its visibility means that a curbside garden will contribute disproportionately to your property's look and feel. Imagine how visitors might relish walking through a garden to get to your front door, or how your mood would lift driving into your garage past a specially designed "welcome home" garden.

A well-designed curbside garden can also cut your chore load. To make it thrive without the mower or trimmer, put in plants that stay the right height, stay in bounds, and stay up year-round. You might end up making a maintenance visit just once or twice a year instead of weekly.

For additional savings in time, effort, and money, make it waterwise. Include only plants that will thrive without supplemental water, or invest in an automated irrigation system to further reduce the resources your curbside landscape will demand every day, every week, every year into the future. Your water bills will drop even as you contribute to the solution.

Don't forget the services a strip of land could provide if cultivated as a garden. It could absorb runoff, grow

Making a powerful impact despite its limited square footage, a parking strip garden transforms the view from the balcony.

food for your family, support woody plants that shelter your home and landscape from sun and wind, provide additional habitat for wildlife, and give a four-season show of texture and color.

Passionate gardeners may run out of room before they run out of passion. If you are an experienced gardener itching for new territory, train your hard-won experience on a tough site and create a well-adapted curbside garden you can be proud of. It might be easier now that you have spent years learning on the rest of your property.

Imagine a world where walking along the street is a delightful sensory experience, parking lots and public grounds refresh the air and water, edibles grow visibly and abundantly, cementscapes are cloaked in foliage, and sun and wind are tempered by still, cool reservoirs of nature. Think how rich life would be if we could move through a public environment savoring its sights, sounds, and aromas.

Your curbside garden brings that world one step closer.

Overview of This Book

You may be discouraged by the challenges and limitations of your curbside space. But the potential rewards—adding precious garden space, meeting neighbors and pedestrians, improving the first impression your home makes, and the sheer thrill of overcoming those challenges with a burst of creativity—could make it worth your while to give that leftover a makeover. This book will guide you gracefully through the process.

In Part 1, Inspirations, explore a coast-to-coast selection of curbside gardens with a variety of styles and situations. Here are solutions for nongardeners and avid gardeners, environmentally conscious citizens and urban farmers.

Part 2, Situations, addresses challenges unique to curbside locations. Learn from other curbside gardeners who have tackled challenges posed by foot, bike, and dog traffic; confronted weed laws and homeowner associations and lived to tell about it; and triumphed over piled snow, leaning signposts, and large trees. Let their strategies and ideas inspire you to give your front yard, alley, parking strip, or other unappealing plot of land a fresh look.

Part 3, Creation, explains how to design, build, and maintain a curbside garden, given the unique properties of these environments. Learn how to build healthy soil, employ earthshaping, design away chores, make a water-wise garden, and more.

Part 4, Curbside-Worthy Plants, offers a list of choice plants for curbside gardens, with information on each plant's needs and behavior to help you choose and combine them effectively. Plants are grouped by their primary contribution: showy flowers, showy foliage, edibles and medicinals, or four-season structure.

left Foodscapes and edible plants like these growing streetside in Portland, Oregon, are popping up in front yards and planting strips from coast to coast.

right A hummingbird contributes as much beauty and interest as the bright patch of nectar-laden flowers it visits.

Throughout the book, when I discuss various situations, I might list a few example plants. My hope is that these examples will shine a light on the vast potential plant choices we have available to us in any region and inspire you to find appropriate choices for your particular site and style. The best way to find plants well suited to your garden is to ask a trusted local expert—a landscape designer, experienced gardener, grower, or staff person at a garden center that sells locally grown plants.

top "And now, we go through my beautiful flower garden," exclaimed the little boy as he pulled his visiting uncle into a magical floral tunnel.

opposite A curbside garden transforms the public sidewalk into a cool, fragrant, pollinator-friendly path.

bottom A hellstrip designed by Lauren Springer Ogden for The Gardens on Spring Creek in Fort Collins, Colorado, showcases an array of tough ground cover plants, including profusely blooming native winecups (*Callirhoe involucrata*) and equally bold mat-forming ice plant (*Delosperma* 'Table Mountain').

PART ONE

Inspirations

Curbside Gardens from Coast to Coast

Sit back, relax, and take an in-depth armchair tour of a dozen inspiring curbside gardens from around the country, chosen to give you a taste of the diverse possibilities. Each garden is a custom blend of people, plants, and place—of art and nature—but wherever you garden, I hope you will find useful ideas, unexpected solutions to your gardening dilemmas, and worthwhile lessons in each of these garden portraits.

A vertically layered and varied plant community inhabits a four-season hellstrip garden in Portland, Oregon.

Cartwheels

Portland, Oregon

Diverse plants thrive on both sides of the public sidewalk, punctuated by concentric diamonds at the garden's entrance.

When Laura Crockett was a shy little girl, she would lure playmates by openly having fun in her front yard—turning cartwheels, riding around on her bike—and other kids would respond to this invitation. Today she does the same thing with her garden, letting it reflect her playful, physical personality. It works, too, she says. "I have met all my best friends because of this garden."

The front yard was entirely lawn when she bought her property seventeen years ago. She laid out a linear garden 8 feet wide on either side of the 75-foot stretch of public sidewalk. One side is the parking strip; the other is bounded by a fence that masks the rest of her front yard.

"I knew I wanted to make a private interior courtyard," she says, "with an obvious, interesting entrance." Her bold geometric design of concentric diamond shapes cuts across the public sidewalk, highlighting a wide gap in her front fence. This opening dramatically frames a large waterfall rushing down a colored concrete wall directly in front of Laura's home.

Laura prefers to see a lot of bloom all at once, so she planned a springtime explosion of color in this garden.

The garden's dramatic formal entrance begins at the street.

It flowers early with abandon in tones that create "high vibrational contrast"—chartreuse donkey tail spurge (*Euphorbia myrsinites*), pink and orange tulips, pink magnolia (*Magnolia* 'Susan'), and drifts of blue woodland phlox (*Phlox divaricata*) and low iris (*Iris pumila* 'Claret').

During other seasons, the garden relies on diverse shapes and textures, and more subtle colors. Laura values the textures above all. "I consider myself a sculptural gardener," she says. Though it is the dreariest time of year for gardens in the Pacific Northwest, her favorite season in this garden is winter, when the evergreens, grasses, and ground covers with year-round foliage play against the varied surfaces of inert materials.

The hardscape's powerful presence adds interest in all seasons. The durable fence of tubular steel and double-walled polycarbonate panels adds a formal, contemporary note. The diamond-shaped paths of packed gray gravel are inset with square, metal-edged stepping-stones filled with recycled glass from yellow traffic lights. Their warm gold brings out orange tones in nearby terra-cotta containers and cut stones.

Metal, glass, and rock delight her not only for their rich textures but also because they gracefully endure her damp climate, where wood is prone to rotting. Her diamond-shaped front bed and glass stepping-stones are edged with steel, cut and welded to shapes she

above left Shafts of low light bathe the garden in full spring bloom.

Iris pumila 'Claret' is part of the springtime explosion of color in this garden.

opposite A path slants across the parking strip. Yellow-toned ground covers swirl around spring tulips nestled in the warm tan foliage of *Carex testacea* 'Prairie Fire'.

specified, installed by a contractor. Steel edges are perfect for a public garden area, she advises. "The corners always stay nice and crisp, even if they get stepped on."

Destruction comes with the territory in public garden areas, and Laura is philosophical about it. After several of her terra-cotta pots were stolen, she devised a way to anchor them in the ground using lengths of steel rebar. Now they stay where she puts them. One year just before Mother's Day, all her flowers were picked. Though she felt very hurt, she chose to imagine that the person who picked them needed a bouquet to give his or her mother. "I have to let go of things out there," she says, "and it's hard, but because it is a public space you cannot get too terribly upset about what happens there."

Laura designs in vertical layers, using both plants and hardscape and relating each layer to those above and below it. Grouped terra-cotta pots rise above chartreuse sedum and blue-green spurge foliage. Abstract arrangements of orange-tinted cut stone pieces spread below masses of blue-flowered perennials. One of her favorite combinations is the alpine totara (*Podocarpus*

nivalis) that stands like an evergreen table below a vase-shaped witch hazel (*Hamamelis ×intermedia* 'Jelena') on the planting strip. She periodically shapes the totara to preserve this effect.

Her sidewalk garden is designed to need minimal care. "About two-thirds to three-quarters of the plants in that garden need no maintenance," she says. These are the slow-growing shrubs and trees that don't require real pruning, just occasional shaping.

In all her designs, Laura uses a maintenance strategy she calls "modified forest floor" to create relatively self-sustaining beds. She lets fallen leaves "rot on the floor" of the garden, and those that fall on the sidewalk are pushed into the beds under woody plants. While decomposing, the leaves feed the soil life, which in turn feeds the plants. This simple technique not only protects the soil from rain compaction but also means Laura does not have to fertilize.

She does no weeding to speak of, either. Now that her plants have filled in, they hold their ground against weeds. Every February she adds a layer of compost, which keeps many unwanted windblown seeds from germinating.

As for trimming, she cuts down the herbaceous plants every June or July, when the springtime perennials have finished blooming. Then yarrow, asters, coneflowers, and summer grasses take over, and she lets them stay up all winter "to provide textural interest and feed the birds and other critters." She cuts them all down in February just as new spring shoots and bulbs emerge, starting the cycle over again.

Laura's garden demonstrates that it is possible to achieve four-season splendor—interesting in every season and changing through the year—using diverse materials without a demanding workload. She sums up her design advice in just five words: "Low maintenance is highly textural."

Small trees with showy blooms

Magnolia 'Susan' makes a lovely small tree, with showy spring flowers and an intoxicating fragrance, for zones 4–8. Try also:

- Texas mountain laurel (*Sophora secundiflora*, zones 7–11) endures hot, drought-ridden summers, and its large, wisteria-like blossoms smell strongly of grape soda.

- Before they leaf out, branches of redbuds are studded with vivid purple-pink, sweetly fragrant blooms. There's a western (*Cercis occidentalis*, zones 7–10) for full sun, an eastern (*C. canadensis*, zones 5–9) for cooler and shadier sites, and a Texas (*C. canadensis* var. *texensis*, zones 6–9) especially for Texans.

Crabapples (here, 'Prairie Fire') contribute to the garden in all four seasons and are some of the best choices for wildlife trees.

- Tall shrub rose of Sharon (*Hibiscus syriacus*, zones 5–8) can be grown as a small multitrunked tree that produces teacup-size flowers all summer and into fall.

- Many varieties of crabapple (*Malus*, zones 4–9, depending on variety) make excellent street trees for urban areas with restricted root zones.

Layers of Leaves

Minneapolis, Minnesota

Hostas are a favorite of northern shade gardeners for their low-care hardiness, showy leaves, and mounding habit.

Jesse Benson's Minneapolis neighborhood boasts many fine old trees that shelter the ground from wind and sun, keep it cooler in summer and warmer in winter, and retain soil moisture with nature's own compost and mulch: layers of fallen leaves. Perhaps because lawns don't grow well in these shady yards but other plants do, the neighborhood is full of gardeners.

When Jesse moved in eight years ago, five mature elms cast deep shade over his front yard, which was consequently filled with hostas. However, soon after he arrived, his leafy canopy succumbed to Dutch elm disease. When the trees went, the birds went as well, and the hosta-loving slugs multiplied unchecked.

Change is a constant in the life of a garden. Taking advantage of the opportunity created by the tree deaths, Jesse has been gradually removing hostas and replacing them with plants that prefer more sun and are less attractive to slugs. He started with several ornamental grasses and a patch of bluestar (*Amsonia*). Quite a few hostas remain, though he has given away many and moved others to his shady back garden. "I've thought about blanching and eating them, they are so abundant," he says seriously.

Jesse layers his plants vertically, placing ground covers and shorter plants underneath taller ones to eliminate bare ground that can attract unwanted seedlings. He has few weeds because his desirable plants are so densely packed.

"People need to be encouraged to plant things close together rather than giving each plant so much space," he says. "There's a flow with planting things through each other. It's important to think about the relationship between plants (and other elements) rather than considering each one separately."

His biggest design challenge has been the narrowness of his parking strip garden. "It's hard to do much because you don't get a chance to create any perspective or sight lines," he explains. He wanted to present plants at eye level where they would be appreciated by people walking past, so he chose some that grow head-high, and he also mounded the earth into a low berm before planting.

His easement contains a not-quite-upright sign about parking regulations; around the signpost he installed a wooden trellis that is anchored in the ground with rebar and can be taken apart and removed should workers need access to the sign. "I gave it all those parallel lines to draw the eye away from the crooked post within," says Jesse.

The trellis provides structure for the garden in the winter, and it contrasts texturally with the billowy plants during the growing season. Not only is it decorative in its own right, but it also supports a striking summer display of lablab vines (*Lablab purpureus*, an annual in this zone 4 garden), their dark-veined foliage festooned with pink flowers and deep purple pods.

In early summer, vivid magenta flowers of hummelo stand out among the varied textures of foliage and seed heads.

opposite, top Annual canna was planted deliberately close so its enormous leaves would grow up through bluestar's feathery foliage.

opposite, bottom Blue switch grass draws a delicate curtain between pedestrians and the street.

The blooms in Jesse's garden take a backseat to the foliage, but flowers in cool shades of pink, blue, and purple add notes of color throughout the growing season. Icy blue bluestar, shell pink penstemon (*Penstemon digitalis*), and sky blue false indigo (*Baptisia australis*) contribute in late spring, followed by deep purple salvia (*Salvia nemorosa*) and magenta hummelo (*Stachys densiflora*). Penstemon's brown seed heads and the dark blue seedpods of false indigo add another season of interest, while the bluestar offers striking gold fall foliage. Best of all, their beauty does not come with a high price tag, as all these perennials are well adapted to Minnesota's climate extremes.

The ornamental grasses green up in early spring and grow tall through the summer, raising their showy seed heads aloft in late summer and autumn. Jesse planted tall feather reed grass (*Calamagrostis acutiflora* 'Karl Foerster') and a blue variety of switch grass (*Panicum*

virgatum), which have similar height and spread but different seed heads to add diverse textures.

In autumn, he rakes the abundant fallen leaves into his garden beds, where they protect his plants through the winter. He lets most stems and seed heads stand because they look good with light snow and hoarfrost. They also provide habitat for smaller mammals.

"A lot of rabbits and mice dart through in the understory of the grass mounds on the parking strip," says Jesse, "and I do anything I can to encourage them to feel comfortable out there." He has found that providing habitat well away from his house can keep small creatures from moving indoors.

"Live and let live" approaches like this can help people address our need to preserve biodiversity, which is crucial for all life including our own. As urban and suburban development continues to devour more wild land and the habitat it provides to all manner of plants and animals, property owners—and gardeners in particular—will have the power to determine which species survive into the future.

In spring, as soon it's warm enough, low creeping phlox and spurge emerge through the leaves on the parking strip and bloom before being overshadowed by taller plants that give a second wave of bloom. Jesse removes some of the leaves in spring but lets the rest stay to feed the soil. He also pushes the leaves back from the sidewalk, making a narrow channel for melting snow and rain to flow into the planting beds. His plants and their leaf mulch soak up the runoff, keeping the paths clearer and safer for the pedestrians, who are suddenly reappearing like green shoots emerging from newly thawed soil.

Lablab vines, low and inconspicuous in spring, attain full glory in late summer.

The fruit of schisandra is known as the five-flavor berry, with elements of all five classic flavors: hot, sour, sweet, salty, and bitter.

Short vines

Annual lablab twines its eye-catching foliage up Jesse's boulevard trellis every year and produces beans that are edible when young (they later accumulate toxins). Try also:

- Schisandra (*Schisandra chinensis*, zones 4–10) drips with red late-summer berries that have been used as a medicinal for centuries.

- Growing to 15 feet, native trumpet honeysuckle (*Lonicera sempervirens*, zones 4–9) attracts hummingbirds, bees, and butterflies with its red-orange flowers.

- Robust, faintly orange-scented native yellow honeysuckle (*Lonicera flava*, zones 4–8) appeals to wrens, chickadees, and other small birds that eat its red berries and nest in its thick foliage.

- Kids love annual firecracker vine (*Ipomoea lobata*), with rainbow rows of warm-hued, puffy flowers that pop like bubble wrap when squeezed.

Urban and Urbane

San Francisco, California

A spare, elegant garden graces an urban row house near a busy corner in San Francisco. The cascading foliage of a peppermint willow (*Agonis flexuosa*) delicately screens the all-glass front door from the street, giving privacy while allowing an unrestricted view of visitors from inside the house. This provides a good balance between sharing the garden and maintaining a more private inner realm.

Though it looks similar to a weeping willow, the peppermint willow makes a much better street tree. It can survive well in a small plot of soil and does not have an aggressive root system as true willows do. It needs moderate water until established and after that can get by with very little. Its crushed foliage smells like peppermint. And perhaps most important for the homeowner, who does all the gardening work himself, it is evergreen and therefore does not drop a lot of leaves.

In fact, every plant in this garden has evergreen foliage, keeping the landscape vibrant throughout the year. Subtle changes mark the passing seasons—a summer spray of shell pink flowers on the coral bells, a sprinkling of white strawberry flowers in spring. "It was not meant to be a flowering garden," says the landscape architect,

Kate Stickley, a partner at Arterra Landscape Architects. "We focused on foliage shape and color for year-round interest."

An orange-leaved New Zealand flax (*Phormium* 'Jester') sports the most colorful foliage in the garden. It reinforces the warm yellow rock tones without outshining the more restrained dark purple coral bells (*Heuchera* 'Crystal Spires' and *H. micrantha* 'Palace Purple') or the neutral gray-green mountain astelia (*Astelia nervosa*). The narrow, pointed leaves of the flax and astelia provide a lively contrast to the ruffled, rounded leaves of the coral bells.

Hardscaping contributes year-round color and texture. In an area prone to frequent fog, warm yellow-toned limestone walls and steps offset the grayness of the weather. A concrete expanse of driveway was remade into "driving strips" of small pavers in reddish-brown hues. "This added planting space helps the driveway blend into the garden and establishes a hierarchy of circulation, so the front door is clearly visible and prominent," explains Kate.

The plants were chosen for their water-thriftiness. "We like low-maintenance, low-water-use landscapes and are very aware of water usage," says Kate. "Most people use 30 to 40 percent more water than their plants need."

above On the parking strip, which sees a lot of traffic from schoolchildren and dog walkers, steppable beach strawberries and purple-leaved coral bells (*Heuchera* 'Crystal Spires') grow thickly around tinted concrete stepping-stones.

opposite Raised beds contribute warm color year-round, reduce maintenance, and add durability.

left The homeowner trims the ground cover by hand to preserve the geometric design.

Irrigation of home landscapes is a way of life for residents of this region and others with summer-dry climates, where typically no rain falls between May and October. In this yard, all of the planted areas are fitted with drip irrigation, and perforated tubes run through the beds of ground covers. The homeowner waters for about thirty minutes three times a week to keep his garden looking healthy. "In sandy soils like this, water percolates though quickly," explains Kate. "Therefore, plants need more frequent watering."

Could dry-climate residents escape the need to irrigate by using only native plants in their landscapes? Theoretically they could, says Kate, but it doesn't work so well with nursery-grown natives. When the plants are accustomed to a certain level of pampering at the nursery, they don't necessarily adapt quickly to a "live or die" setting in an unirrigated landscape. She suggests that homeowners who bring native plants home from the nursery irrigate them to help them settle in, "then grad-

ually dial the water back to find the tipping point, and up it slightly from there and see if that does it." Using less water is best, as it will prolong the lives of native plants; if overwatered, they may grow faster and die sooner.

Another issue in summer-dry climates is that all the precipitation comes in the winter. If that water isn't absorbed into the landscape, surges of runoff from roofs and paved areas can cause water pollution, shoreline erosion, fish kill, and other environmental problems. Homeowners can make a big difference by replacing some of their paved areas with more permeable pavement and garden space, like this home's more absorbent driveway. Using evergreen plants also helps soak up more winter runoff, because they are actively growing and taking up water during the rainy season.

Evergreens suit this garden's peaceful mood, carefully cultivated to offset its bustling setting. Rock planters flanking the front entrance create a formal and orderly facade. The restricted color palette brings cohesion

Gray concrete with a few sheared shrubs dominates this front yard before the makeover.

and calm. Compact green foliage of beach strawberries (*Fragaria chiloensis*) flows serenely around mounding plants, tying different parts of the garden together.

The garden requires regular attention to preserve its tidy serenity. The homeowner spends about two hours a month clipping ground covers by hand. "The yard work is more than I anticipated," he says, "but if it is done regularly it can be pleasant to be outside."

Located in a walkable area near a school, this small front garden was altruistically designed to create a pleasing experience for pedestrians. "Rather than closing off such a small garden, we wanted to make it a place that could stand a lot of neighborhood activity," says Kate. "The ground covers can handle foot traffic, and the wall is for sitting."

"Occasionally older people out for a little exercise use the rock walls to sit on," says the homeowner, "and of course the schoolchildren find the curb 'steps' irresistible to play a little hopscotch. Can't argue with that."

Small low-litter trees

The aromatic, evergreen peppermint willow is a rare treasure. Here are several deciduous low-mess options:

- Green-trunked, fragrant-flowering palo verde (*Parkinsonia aculeata*, zones 8–11) acts as a "nurse tree" for young saguaro cacti, sheltering them from intense sun and heat.

- Mountain ash (*Sorbus aucuparia*, zones 3–6) boasts bright orange berries that migrating birds devour, if you don't gather them first to make rowanberry schnapps.

- Medium-sized at 30 to 40 feet tall, seedless varieties of honey locust (*Gleditsia triacanthos* f. *inermis*, zones 3–8) tolerate pollution, wind, salt, and drought, and cast

Combined berries and fall color of mountain ash 'Joseph Rock' make a splash.

light shade over urban gathering spots.

- Desert willow (*Chilopsis linearis*, zones 6–9), a small native desert tree with fragrant pink flowers, attracts hummingbirds all summer.

A Meadow Mood

Boulder, Colorado

Unmortared stone paths branch off the main walk, one leading through a shady garden and the other a sunny one.

Native grasses, perennials, sedges, shrubs, and creeping ground covers weave an ever-changing tapestry of texture and color across Bobbi and Tim Carlin's large front yard in Boulder, Colorado.

"It's different during each season," says Bobbi. "That's one of the things we love about it! Something is always in bloom except in the dead of winter, and most everything, whether blooming or not, is interesting."

"Landscaping is the best money we have spent," Tim adds. "I see new things every time I come out here."

The couple enlisted nationally known garden designers Lauren Springer Ogden and Scott Ogden to transform their lawn and foundation plants into a waterwise garden suited to the challenging conditions of North America's intermountain region. Bobbi had taken several of Lauren's landscaping classes. "The classes absolutely changed my ideas of what I wanted for my own garden," she recalls. "I didn't realize how a garden could look fantastic year-round."

The Ogdens kept several existing trees near the house but removed a large blue spruce out at the curb.

They replaced the lawn with a low, naturalistic mix of xeric plants and rearranged existing shrubs and boulders within it. Their intent was to mimic the wild Colorado landscape above the tree line, with its wide open spaces and views, where Bobbi enjoys hiking.

Two auxiliary paths of unmortared stepping-stones were added off the existing mortared stone front walk. One of the new paths leads through the garden to the driveway, and the other cuts through a shadier area to wrap around the side of the house. Walkable plants—

Lauren Ogden (left) and Bobbi Carlin survey the Carlins' typical suburban yard before retrofitting with a waterwise landscape.

opposite The Ogdens kept existing trees, shrubs, and boulders and converted the lawn to a regionally appropriate mix of native and other dry-adapted plants, making a vivid and dynamic year-round landscape.

dwarf pussytoes (*Antennaria parvifolia*), Turkish veronica (*Veronica liwanensis*), and creeping thymes—spill onto the path from cracks between paving stones. These unmortared paths are Bobbi's favorite feature of the garden. "They have lovely little ground covers growing between the stones, and no matter how much I trample them or run wheelbarrows over them, they continue to expand and bloom."

Two years after the garden was created, the plants are already filling in and choreographing a year-round show. The sunny path curves through an astonishingly diverse meadow of grasses, flowers, and occasional shrubs and boulders. Bulbs emerge from ground covers that mingle through taller plants and will eventually cover all bare soil. Lauren advocates vertical layering, a common practice in woodland gardens that works well in drought-tolerant meadow gardens too. Instead of individual plants separated by empty space in a carefully controlled layout, "they kind of duke it out like plants grow in nature," she says. "Close planting doesn't promote fungal disease here," she adds. "There's enough wind and sun, and the plants just blow around together."

This strategy of mulching with plants rather than wood chips or gravel is one of the things Bobbi liked the best about Lauren's approach, and something she knew she wanted for her own garden. "I don't like the look of gravel, and wood chips make no sense in Colorado—it's too windy. I used to spend time in the summer putting them down and then all winter and spring sweeping them up! I love every inch of dirt being covered with plants that 'knit together,' as Lauren would say."

Below the front porch, in the shade of an existing ash tree, low mounding plants that grow well in filtered light—variegated coral bells (a *Heuchera* variety), Siberian bugloss (*Brunnera macrophylla*), a sedge or two (*Carex* species), wild ginger (*Asarum europaeum*), plumbago (*Ceratostigma plumbaginoides*), peach-leaved bellflower (*Campanula persicifolia*)—make a rolling carpet of varied textures and colors. "I grew up on the East Coast, and I miss that green, woodsy feeling," says Bobbi. "The shade areas are just that for me. It amazes me they can look so lush here with so little water and effort." These plants are not as water-thrifty as those in the sunny area, notes Lauren. "Most shade gardens require quite a bit of extra water in our region because shade plants evolved in forest ecosystems that receive twice or more the annual rainfall that our semi-desert steppe climate receives."

This area really expands the garden's biodiversity, but it also presented the biggest design challenge. "It's hard to visually integrate plantings for shade and sun so close together," Lauren explains. She used grasses and sedges to tie different areas together and make the design read as a continuous landscape. Grasses are helpful fillers, and their presence reduces maintenance in a garden. A planting of flowers without grasses is less interesting visually too, because it lacks textural variety. Lauren likes the shimmery, moving textures of the grasses. "They lend a feel that's not so plastic."

Though Lauren would not describe the entire garden as a low-water landscape (the sunny areas qualify, but not the shaded ones), the Carlins are delighted that they are saving water in addition to getting a year-round landscape. "Colorado is in the midst of a drought," says Bobbi, "but we'll still have a wonderful-looking front yard, using much less water than a lawn."

The garden is watered by the same irrigation system the Carlins used on their lawn; the heads were simply retrofitted with pop-up sprinklers that reach above the plants, which are a little taller than turf. They use the sprinkler system once a week at most in the extreme heat of the summer, much less often during the rest of the growing season. In contrast, Colorado lawns are typically watered three times a week. Bobbi manually waters new plants and those that need more water. It takes more time than just flipping a switch, she admits, but it saves a lot of water and she likes to be out in the garden.

Because they chose well-adapted plants and started with healthy soil, they don't fertilize. "Unlike eastern perennials that are bigger feeders, intermountain plants prefer a slow release of nutrients. There's little natural

top Red-flowering pinestemon (front and center) and dozens of other species mingle in this diverse, sunny stretch of the garden, shown in its second summer.

In autumn, seed heads of big blue grama (*Bouteloua gracilis* 'Blonde Ambition'), butterfly weed (*Asclepias tuberosa*), and 'Undaunted' ruby muhly (*Muhlenbergia reverchonii*), a 2014 Plant Select introduction by Lauren and Scott Ogden, steal the spotlight.

The touchably furred, two-toned leaves and low, dense habit of roundleaf horehound (*Marrubium rotundifolium*) make it an excellent pathside plant.

nitrogen in this soil, and they're well adapted to that," explains Lauren. "Rather than using fertilizers and amending soil, the biggest issue for me is to jump-start the microbial action." She does this by making sure the soil is aerated, and sometimes she'll broadcast alfalfa pellets for a mild boost of organic matter. This wasn't necessary in the Carlins' yard, where her main concern was to keep their existing soil structure intact. "We planted small plants so we could dig small holes. We even left the dead grass to attract microbial life as it slowly decomposed. It brought so many worms it was almost disgusting—it's like spaghetti."

The garden needs just one spring cleanup and small trimmings through the year. Quite a few plants stay evergreen and need no cutting—pineleaf penstemon (*Penstemon pinifolius*), dwarf conifers, all the ground covers, cotoneaster. "We didn't include self-sowers, which reduces the maintenance needed," says Lauren, "but Bobbi does cut certain things back and leaves others standing for their aesthetic value."

Plants in this climate grow "lean and mean," so they don't generate as much debris as the large drifts of bold perennials that have become more common in wetter regions' lawnless landscapes. It's more sustainable if you don't generate large amounts of trimmings, says Lauren, unless you have municipal composting that can take that waste and convert it to compost for use in area gardens. Also it's more sustainable in that you can continue maintaining the garden throughout your life. Masses of tall perennials are beautiful, but "if you're eighty years old, who's going to cut them back for you?"

An advocate of educating homeowners about landscape maintenance before they convert lawn to garden, Lauren stresses that this is not a care-free landscape to be installed and ignored. "Bobbi is a natural. She actually wants to garden, and she knows how to care for the plants to keep it looking good year-round. I have very few clients who can do this well without professional help, and often the professionals aren't very good at it either."

Bobbi enjoys the variety and seasonality of tasks that go along with maintaining her new garden. "I must say, it is more work than a lawn," she admits, "but I love gardening and don't find the upkeep daunting. At certain times of the year I need to weed, at other times I need to trim, at other times I need to clean up. And as things knit together, there's less and less weeding to do."

Large-leaved silver-tinted ground covers

Leaves of roundleaf horehound are gray-green on top and woolly white underneath, giving a silvery effect. Try also:

- Big-leaf pussytoes (*Antennaria plantaginifolia*, zones 3–8) forms a felted mat of ovate white-green leaves, then extends 6-inch stems with fuzzy white flowers that look like curled cats' paws.

- If you prefer a bird theme, the overlapping white furry leaves of low-growing partridge feather (*Tanacetum densum*, zones 4–9) look like tiny feathers.

- Trailing stems of silver ponyfoot (*Dichondra argentea*, zones 9–11)

A living mulch of silver ponyfoot surrounds clumps of Mexican feather grass (*Nassella tenuissima*) at Lady Bird Johnson Wildflower Center in Austin, Texas.

form a looser carpet of small, bluish silver dollars.

- Can't commit? Tender perennial licorice plant (*Helichrysum petiolare*, zones 9–11), grown as an annual, drapes its foliage gracefully down the sides of a container.

A vignette alongside the driveway—one chord in this magnum opus—pairs low blue fingers of curlicue sage (*Artemisia versicolor* 'Sea Foam') with taller spikes of dotted blazing star (*Liatris punctata*) seed heads and a cloud of big blue grama above.

Tiny Jewel

Buffalo, New York

Of the bed of ornamental grasses visible from her new front stoop, Karen Tashjian says approvingly, "You feel like you're in a cornfield or something."

"I like to make space," says Buffalo-based architect Karen Tashjian. When she took on the renovation of a modest older home, she was primarily focused on indoor space. Her first major outdoor decision was choosing a house color that would work well with the neighbor's scheme of brilliant orange; she settled on a "gentle response" of deep blue.

Another key choice—the one that really started the garden—was her decision to dismantle a rotting front porch. She replaced it with a smaller portico around the front entrance, and this opened up the possibility and the space for an outdoor living area. What a luxury in this neighborhood of tiny front yards, says Karen, where "many times gardens are just the face on a house." Using architectural principles to determine a pleasing shape and scale, she marked off an outdoor living area in the middle of the yard.

Thanks to a birthday gift from her husband, she was able to engage a garden consultant to help her create planted areas around the new outdoor room. First they removed the top 4 inches of compacted and nutrient-poor urban soil and replaced it with high-quality topsoil.

Karen Tashjian's dyed concrete "welcome mat" marks the entrance to both outdoor and indoor living spaces.

Then, to go with the blue house, they made a blue garden. Paler-blooming bluestar (*Amsonia*) complements the deeper-hued flowers of perennial salvia (*Salvia nemorosa*) and iris. Blue oat grass (*Helictotrichon sempervirens*) and hostas contribute blue foliage, while companion plants provide different color accents: pink chives, darker pink peonies, and cream-colored seed heads of English lavender (*Lavandula angustifolia*).

Karen planted more plants and closer together than the recommended spacing because she wanted them to fill in quickly. Her only regret was including so many daisies in the garden; they grew so tall and numerous that their boisterous white flowers distract from the soothing blueness.

The open space that she carefully designed was covered with a layer of pea gravel to make an informal patio. Unfortunately, neighborhood cats mistook all that fresh gravel for a king-sized litter box, which created a real maintenance challenge. Karen spread mothballs around the gravel to no avail. Then, while out buying granite for the new kitchen counter, she noticed a commercial dumpster full of granite pieces. "A little slippery but wonderful to walk on," they made ideal paving stones for the patio. Not only did it give her a glow to rescue waste from other projects, but also the stones made the area less interesting to neighborhood cats.

In the garden as well as the house, Karen chose to do a lot of the labor herself, and she made it a priority to reuse and recycle materials as much as possible. In addition to diverting perfectly good granite from the waste stream, she edged the planting beds with repurposed bricks taken from an obsolete chimney that was removed from the house. Other materials were scavenged from local curbsides and even trash bins.

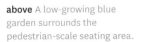 **above** A low-growing blue garden surrounds the pedestrian-scale seating area.

Scrapped granite pieces and creeping plants cover the floor of this outdoor room, furnished with salvaged chairs.

Dismantling the porch left a hole in the front walk, which she filled with a blue concrete "threshold" at the foot of the new portico steps. "It's totally my invention," she says. The concrete was stained with a blue dye, and she embedded tiny glass tiles to make it sparkle.

A hedge of mature shrubs ranged along the main walkway of the house, and though it bestowed a welcome feeling of privacy and enclosure, she followed her design intuition and removed it. Replacing it with shorter plants blended her garden with her neighbor's garden, and somehow that made the space more comfortable. She searches for words to explain: "It created a bigger effect with more of a vista."

Pedestrian-scale outdoor spaces like her new garden just feel good, she adds, pointing to adjacent Summer Street. A highlight of Buffalo's famous annual Garden Walk, the street features minuscule front gardens, balconies, window boxes, and planted parking strips. These scores of tiny, diverse, publicly visible garden areas create a powerful effect; together, they diminish the role of the street and expand the community space and presence. "There's a human scale to that whole street that I just love, that invites more personal interaction between neighbors," Karen says. "You can stand on your doorstep and speak in a normal voice to someone on the street. This is special."

When Karen completed her renovation and put the house up for sale, her garden was only two and a half years old, and the main upkeep required was "weeding and picking garbage out." The plants had filled in enough that she thinned them, and of course she repurposed the excess plants, taking away the beginnings of another blue garden.

Nick Heim, who bought the newly updated house, says he and his wife love "our little urban garden nook";

though a novice gardener, he has already gotten his hands dirty moving a few plants around.

Meanwhile, Karen Tashjian was hired as an architect to renovate another home down the street. She sees this as a vindication of her methods and of her belief that sensitive renovation of an existing structure, in tune with its style and surroundings, adds value to the entire neighborhood. She'd love to take on more projects like this one, where "I could do it artistically, and I could reuse materials for a very green experience."

Mounds of blue flowers

Bluestar contributes fine texture, pale blue spring flowers, and golden fall color. Try also:

- With delicate looks and inner toughness, Russian sage (*Perovskia atriplicifolia*, zones 4–9) wafts a blue mist of bloom over inhospitable sites.

- Plant creeping Jacob's ladder (*Polemonium reptans*, zones 3–8) in wooded areas or on the east side of a building; it's good for bees and trees.

- Bluebeard (*Caryopteris*, zones 5–9), a low, rounded shrub, contributes structure and texture long after its fragrant, fuzzy blue flower clusters have faded.

A skirt of bluebeard (*Caryopteris ×clandonensis* 'Worcester Gold') hides the legs of variegated boxleaf honeysuckle (*Lonicera nitida* 'Lemon Beauty'), with creamy flower spikes of variegated Spanish dagger (*Yucca gloriosa* 'Variegata') rising up from behind.

- Scores of wild geranium cultivars (*Geranium*, zones 3–8) produce abundant single blue flowers and bold, lobed foliage with red-pink-orange autumn color.

Seed heads and flowers bob around your knees when you're seated on the patio.

Fire and Water

Seattle, Washington

During that grayest season in a climate of grays, warm and fiery tones paint a dramatic winter scene.

Dan Corson and Berndt Stugger met a lot of people as they were creating their small urban garden in Seattle. "At the beginning, we were out there all the time," Berndt recalls. "There was hardly a way to pass by without interacting with us."

The couple bought their house in 2000 and started on the garden right away. Installing the plants and keeping bare spots weeded was an intense job at first. They practiced "extreme gardening," wearing headlamps to lengthen the days and squeeze in a bit more work. However, once the plants grew dense enough to cover the ground, the workload dropped dramatically. Now they spend about two weekends in fall and two in the spring on garden cleanup, with maintenance averaging a paltry half an hour a month during the rest of the year.

Dan, a sculptor by training, treated the plants as his medium and massed them into interesting, evocative forms. "So many gardens are focused on onesy-twosy plantings," he explains. "I wanted large drifts of plants and sculptural landscaping." Inspired by the rippling patterns of Japanese raked gravel gardens, waves of black

mondo grass (*Ophiopogon planiscapus* 'Nigrescens'), Japanese forest grass (*Hakonechloa macra* 'Aureola'), and chartreuse sedum roll across their front yard. A river of lavender (*Lavandula ×intermedia* 'Grosso') cuts a dramatic swath, continuing across the sidewalk.

The garden's powerful imagery—part Hawaii, part Mount Saint Helens—unleashes the imagination. Its intriguing patterns and forms bring to mind flowing lava, cascading water, patches of snow and ice, and burning torches.

However, that power comes with a downside. Strictly adhering to their pattern means these avid gardeners can't include many plants they wish to grow. "Resisting a new plant is the highest form of willpower," agrees Dan. For instance, their deliberately spaced foxtail lilies (*Eremerus* 'Cleopatra') make splendid torches, but that effect would be confused were they to include other torchlike blooms such as red hot poker (*Kniphofia*) or blazing star (*Liatris*). When they end up with a plant that doesn't fit their garden, he confides, they offer it to the neighbors across the street in hopes that they can still enjoy it.

Like most established gardens, this one has undergone a certain amount of trial and error to find well-suited plants. One challenge in the Pacific Northwest is the region's cool springs. Plants can be slow starters here if they need warmer soil temperatures to resume growth after winter dormancy. The men made several attempts before they found a chartreuse plant that would look good year-round and bounce back quickly each spring,

This garden uses sculptural landscaping; plants are grouped to create bold, evocative forms and patterns.

rejecting both golden creeping speedwell (*Veronica repens* 'Sunshine') and golden Japanese stonecrop (*Sedum makinoi* 'Ogon') before settling on 'Angelina' stonecrop (*Sedum rupestre* 'Angelina'). And it still isn't ideal: though its foliage performs well, the bright yellow flowers stick up and spoil the effect for Dan, so he clips them off.

In this walkable neighborhood, their curbside garden sees plenty of pedestrians. The river of lavender that crosses their sidewalk invites interaction. "People will walk by and stroke those flowers," says Dan, though some get nervous when they notice the humming cloud of pollinators. Those who want to avoid touching the plants can stick to the center of the sidewalk.

While the lawn on the parking strip next door gets plenty of canine action (both walking and squatting),

Dan and Berndt's garden remains fairly unscathed. They suspect that the garden's clear, intentional design may prompt dog walkers to steer their dogs elsewhere.

Also, their abundance of shrubs makes a four-season dog deterrent. Twiggy heather (*Calluna vulgaris* 'Wickwar Flame') covers the parking strip under the taller witch hazel (*Hamamelis ×intermedia* 'Arnold Promise'), while a mounded bed of black mondo erupts with blood-twig dogwood (*Cornus sanguinea* 'Midwinter Fire'). But these shrubs are not merely utilitarian; they contribute mightily to the garden's beauty, making their boldest design statement in winter.

The most challenging area of the garden is an occasional parking space that the men created by replacing their concrete slab driveway with flagstones interplanted

right Occasional foxtail lilies recall the lit torches of a Hawaiian resort.

below Flamelike dogwood stems flicker above a ground cover of black mondo grass, its dark tint suggesting scorched earth or cooled molten lava.

with mini mondo (*Ophiopogon japonicus* 'Nanus') and other low plants. This sparsely planted area is more vulnerable to windborne weeds, mainly neighbors' lawn grasses gone to seed. Since Dan and Berndt don't use herbicides (or any pesticides) in their landscape, this means more time spent pulling grass seedlings from between pavers.

Not only has their garden profoundly influenced their immediate environment, it has also helped them settle in and put down their own roots. "Our garden has connected us to our neighbors and our community more than any single other thing we have done," says Dan. "We know five times the number of passing people that our nongardening friends do." The couple renews those connections every year by gifting their neighbors with hundreds of bundles of lavender clipped from their garden.

top "We wanted off-street parking that didn't look like it," says Dan Corson, and indeed, new visitors don't usually park here because they assume it's part of the garden.

A ghostly vignette featuring big-leaved silver sage (*Salvia argentea*), feathery *Artemisia schmidtiana* 'Silver Mound', and lamb's ear *Stachys byzantina* rests like a patch of ice or frothing eddy beside the lavender river.

Torchlike blooms

Foxtail lilies supply a glowing, torchlike bloom all summer in sites with rich, moist soil. Try also:

- An assortment of blazing star species (*Liatris*, zones 3–9) native to different regions across the continent produce summer spikes of magenta flowers that host clouds of butterflies.

- In areas with cooler summers, hybrid varieties of lupine (*Lupinus ×hybrida*, zones 4–8) make towers of flowers, yellow to pink to blue to white; scatter the seeds to keep them coming.

- Red hot poker (*Kniphofia*, zones 5–9 depending on variety)

Standing in an edible-berried carpet of creeping bramble (*Rubus calycinoides*), pale yellow red hot poker shines against the dark foliage of smokebush (*Cotinus coggygria* 'Royal Purple') in a Portland, Oregon, hellstrip.

produces sturdy stalks with tight-clustered flowers in yellow to red tones, some two-toned, all hot.

- Perennial straw foxglove (*Digitalis lutea*, zones 3–9) raises pale yellow torches under trees in sites sheltered from afternoon sun.

Everyone Welcome
Minneapolis, Minnesota

Silver-leaved African daisy (*Gazania* 'Talent Orange') makes a heatproof walkway edger, backed by drifts of colorful coleus cultivars and lacy flower heads of clump-forming fleeceflower (*Persicaria polymorpha*).

"It's exciting to work with a place that celebrates everything local," says Scott Endres, whose company redesigned the landscaping around the Seward Co-op, a member-owned grocery store in Minneapolis. "It needed bolder brushstrokes," he said. "The garden has to compete with the loudness of the city around it." He's referring to visual loudness; located on a busy main road in a thriving urban community, the co-op is surrounded by tall residential and commercial buildings. In addition to round-the-clock car traffic, the garden sees a parade of cyclists and pedestrians with skin tones and clothing in a rainbow of colors.

The roughly 3000-square-foot garden is distributed around the edges of the property, alongside the public sidewalks. Narrow but diverse planting beds frame the west and north sides of the bustling parking lot, vertically layered with a mix of perennials, annuals, grasses, and even a few vines twining through the sturdy metal fence, all forming a lush understory to several young maple trees (*Acer ×freemanii* 'Autumn Blaze', a hybrid of red and silver maple).

The goal was to add more visual oomph to the garden, especially when viewed from a distance. Scott's team rearranged the diverse mix of native perennials, clustering plants of each species to emphasize their textures, colors, and forms. Now groups of New England aster (*Symphyotrichum novae-angliae*), a compact form of smooth oxeye (*Heliopsis helianthoides*), and Joe Pye weed (*Eutrochium purpureum* 'Little Joe') repeat throughout the garden, knitting it together.

He also introduced bold foliage in the form of decorative annuals and edibles, including multiple varieties of kale (*Brassica oleracea*), coleus (*Solenostemon*), African daisy (*Gazania*), and copperleaf (*Acalypha wilkesiana*). "Flowers come and go, but foliage will be there all season," he says. Such a visible and public garden needs to be as beautiful as possible at every time of year.

Are annual plants worth the extra work of planting them anew each spring and removing them in the fall? Absolutely they are, says Scott. Annuals are "the exclamation points" that add constant beauty, and they often make additional contributions such as vigor, color, and

edibility. The annuals keep it fun and exciting because every year you can discover new combinations. "You may create a winning combination that is just a beautiful memory next year when you find new ones," he says. In addition, removing the dead plants creates pockets that make it easier to amend soil or divide perennials.

Scott often encourages clients to scatter annuals among their perennials for a better show. A few well-chosen annuals can really spice up a low-maintenance landscape or a native plant garden. They add diversity, which is not only aesthetically pleasing but also useful for confusing pests and reducing the spread of disease. "I think a lot of the things we do in cultivated gardens are compromises," he says, ways to balance aesthetics with stewardship of the planet.

He compares creating a sustainable but arrestingly beautiful garden with crafting a delicious soup from local ingredients. If you restrict yourself to using only the vegetables harvested from your garden every season, you might have a fairly limited repertoire during some seasons. Imagine the improvement when you have something special stored up that can add a real kick to that soup—a splash of cognac, exotic spices, or balsamic vinegar. The few nonlocal ingredients powerfully boost the soup's flavor and your own enjoyment.

Scott's company, Tangletown Gardens, has developed earth-friendly processes for incorporating annuals into their clients' gardens. They use local plants grown at their nearby farm, maintained using organic fertilizers, compost, and earth-friendly pest controls such as insecticidal soap and insect predators. Spent annuals are not treated as a waste product but as a key ingredient for maintaining healthy gardens. Plants pulled from clients' urban gardens are returned to the farm for composting (in the case of Seward Co-op, they also take food wastes)

above Diverse plantings embody the Seward Co-op's motto: "Everyone Welcome."

Bold foliage plants include eye-catching 'Redbor' kale.

opposite A stately combination of annual cattail millet (*Pennisetum glaucum* 'Purple Majesty') and perennial Joe Pye weed anchors one corner of the parking lot.

and each spring, finished compost is distributed to clients' gardens. In this way, clients with no space for—or no interest in—making compost can still be part of the natural cycle of soil building, both contributing to and benefiting from it.

Seward Co-op's landscape aims not only to beautify the neighborhood but also to be waterwise. Drip irrigation was installed throughout the gardens around the parking lot. "It helps new plants to establish and combats our reality of weather extremes," Scott explains, and it can be adjusted as plants' needs change.

Along the south (and lowest) edge of the parking lot, a gravel-covered French drain carries runoff into a rain garden behind the building, bursting with native tallgrass prairie plants that partly hide the building wall from neighboring houses. Roof drain spouts empty into it as well.

Tangletown Gardens staff visit the Seward Co-op garden weekly during the growing season to keep it looking good. Maintenance chores include planting, trimming dead or damaged parts, and removing dead annuals and unhealthy plants, as well as ongoing soil amendment and rearranging. They don't mulch the garden; thick planting holds the soil against erosion and conserves soil moisture.

Customers have been enthusiastic about the co-op's vivid plantings, says Scott. "They always have great compliments. When our staff are out tending the garden, it's a love-fest."

Bold-leaved edible greens

Texturally appealing kale makes a delicious statement in the border and on the plate. Try also:

- Radicchio (*Cichorium intybus*) adds an agreeably bitter flavor to salads, soups, and grain dishes. If harvested correctly, heads can be regrown several times from the same plant.

- The sour and succulent green foliage of perennial sorrel (*Rumex acetosa*, zones 3–9) delivers deliciousness year after year.

- Mustards (*Brassica juncea*) emerge early and linger, with heavily textured foliage of deep purple to red that is edible raw, steamed, or sautéed.

Spicy red-veined radicchio, available in a multitude of leaf colors and patterns, livens up any border with its dramatic form, color, and texture—and then you eat it.

- Perennial hostas (zones 3–9, depending on variety) are edible; their young shoots have a mild flavor well known in Japanese cuisine and familiar to adventurous palates in other parts of the world. They are also a delicacy to slugs, rabbits, and deer.

above Tender perennial copperleaf (*Acalypha wilkesiana* 'Louisiana Red') adds summer spice to this heavily trafficked curbside garden.

Tuscan kale (also known as lacinato or dinosaur kale) is the highest-quality culinary kale. It tolerates extreme heat and cold, and its puckered blue-green foliage looks good from spring through Thanksgiving in Minnesota.

On the Sunny Side

Charlotte, North Carolina

Foxgloves (*Digitalis purpurea*), larkspur, poppies, and *Rosa* 'Belinda's Dream' make an enchanting cottage combination.

Famed garden writer Elizabeth Lawrence used her North Carolina garden as a living laboratory and an inspiration for her writings over several decades. Lindie Wilson, already an accomplished gardener, gave herself a world-class gardening education when she purchased the property and stewarded it for two decades before placing it in a conservation easement held by the Garden Conservancy. It is now owned and operated by Wing Haven Foundation as an educational garden open to the public, preserving Miss Lawrence's legacy for future generations of garden lovers.

Like the Elizabeth Lawrence Garden, Lindie's current property is a lawnless stroll garden. Multiple paths beckon explorers through expansive planted areas. The front garden is only three years old but is entirely laid out and planted. From the curb, a wide central walk leads directly to the front door, cut by symmetric cul-de-sac paths near the street and a narrow path crossing the property near the house.

Lindie learned from Elizabeth Lawrence the usefulness of having a formal design. "You could sort of

Comfortably wide crushed stone paths allow plants to arch naturally.

right At the height of bloom, pink poppies strew glowing blossoms across the garden, and the blue spires of larkspur burst up through the foliage of other plants.

go crazy with the plants, because her beautiful garden design was there and it held things together," she says. And Lindie does like going crazy with the plants. Stewarding her previous garden meant restricting herself to historically accurate plants and those adapted to shady conditions, but toward the end of her stay, anticipation got the best of her. "I'm unfortunately a serious plantaholic," she confesses. "I would buy things and keep them in a pot." By the time she bought her current property, she had already accumulated quite a few plants for it.

Her tastes embrace old-fashioned cottage flowers, herbs with colorful foliage, annuals, biennials, perennials, shrubs, edibles, and even a few well-behaved vines on decorative metal towers. Carefully chosen roses grow among the plant-packed communities—not set apart as so many roses are, but intertwined with other plants to make intriguing combinations of shapes, textures, and colors. "The only roses out there are very tough ones that don't require spraying," says Lindie.

Rosa 'Belinda's Dream', a new favorite, has tightly bunched petals that form gorgeous full-headed blooms the pearly pink color of strawberry ice cream. "It also

looks great in July when it's 95 out there, it repeats, and it's good for cut flowers." Bright pink, single-flowered *Rosa mutabilis* also made the grade, though she must chop it back every few years to keep it to its allotted space. After decades of shade gardening, Lindie is adamant that her front garden will remain sunny, so she limits her woody plants to those of manageable size and habit.

Her mix of plants changes every year because she includes a good proportion of annuals, some self-sown and others planted out in spring. "I really depend on a lot of annuals—particularly silver and yellow variegated salvia varieties—to make my garden beautiful in fall," she says. "I carry them over from cuttings in my greenhouse." These late-blooming winter annuals are a time-honored practice of southern gardeners, extending the season of color up to the onset of frost.

When Lindie arrived, her current front yard was a "blank slate of bermudagrass." A hired landscaper killed the lawn by spraying it in midsummer during its peak growth. They laid out her paths of local crushed stone directly onto the dead lawn. "Elizabeth Lawrence used it, and I liked it so much that I used it here. It's finer to walk on than gravel," she says. It gradually compacts over time, so she will top up her paths with a new layer every few years.

Where the beds would be, they covered the dead grass with 6 or 7 inches of compost made by the city from collected yard waste. Though organic gardeners may avoid it because it could contain nonorganic wastes, "It's really, really broken down, and it's like black gold." It is the perfect conditioner for Lindie's red clay soil, which "is awful and sticky and dense and hard to work with, but when you amend it with compost, it's very fertile and holds moisture and grows things well."

above Hip-high rue (*Ruta graveolens*)—with acid yellow flowers and lacy foliage—and aromatic, edible black fennel (*Foeniculum vulgare* 'Purpureum') supply color for the garden and larval food for butterflies.

right Arborvitae (*Thuja occidentalis* 'Degroot's Spire') is one of the few evergreens that can endure North Carolina summers unscathed.

opposite 'Climax' blueberries ripen along the edge of the driveway.

The plants in her young garden are not merely growing; they are proliferating. Her spring-blooming annuals—poppies (*Papaver somniferum*), larkspur (*Consolida*), love-in-a-mist (*Nigella damascena*)—are great self-sowers. "That's the one thing that has really gotten out of control," she muses. She uses different strategies to manage this abundance, with varying success—clipping spent blooms before they form seed heads, adding a light mulch of leaf mold in late fall to reduce germination, and cutting down all herbaceous plants in early winter after birds have foraged on the seed heads. And still, plenty of seedlings sprout for each year's show.

The entire garden is watered thoroughly every two weeks in summer when there has been no rain. Lindie uses overhead sprinklers to achieve good coverage of her tall, dense plantings. New plants are watered manually for their first couple of years, once a week if there has not been an inch of rain.

The garden gets much less water than a lawn would demand in her climate. In fact, fescue lawns won't stay green during her region's scorching summers, even with copious watering. Lindie is among a growing group of Charlotte area gardeners who are reducing their lawns. "People are going to have to change," she says matter-of-factly. "They won't be able to afford the water."

Decorative shrubs with edible fruit

Blueberries, with their early white bell-shaped flowers, delicious fruits, and red-orange fall foliage, make great front-of-the-border plants. Try also:

- Grow your own indoor air freshener; plant clove currants (*Ribes odoratum*, zones 4–8) on damp, shady sides of buildings, then open the windows when they flower.

- Waist high and prickly, gooseberries (*Ribes hirtellum*, zones 3–8) also grow well on the north sides of buildings, where they provide burglar-proofing under windows.

Blooming clove currant wafts its spicy scent indoors through open windows in spring, but you must step outside in summer to graze on the sweet black berries.

- Southwestern native Fendler's barberry (*Berberis fendleri*, zones 3–8) produces red edible fruit that tastes like a sweet cranberry, as well as fall color, and is not invasive like its Japanese cousin (*Berberis thunbergii*).

Serenity in the City
Boise, Idaho

The planted berm is tall enough to screen out cars and pavement but still allow a borrowed view of mature trees in the park across the street.

Jessica Cortright and Hans Germann transformed their tiny urban front yard into a private outdoor haven equally suited to a lone thinker or an intimate gathering of friends. Their maintenance-free deck is surrounded by grasses and flowers. A Yoshino cherry tree (*Prunus ×yedoensis*) spreads a protective ceiling of leaves overhead. The scenery changes through the seasons and entices year-round.

Because their work leaves little time for coddling a traditional lawn or a demanding landscape, Jessica set out to "create a comfortable space that didn't require any maintenance at all." She designed and built the garden with the help of Hans and her brother, Gerry. They rented a skid-steer loader and backhoe, scraped off the topsoil from much of the front yard, and used it to create a berm with deep, rich, fertile soil across the front of the property. Then they installed the deck over most of the remaining front yard. They also laid flagstone-and-gravel paths and sawed lengths of railroad ties to create durable edging.

Around the sitting area, Jessica placed special stones. Each rock has its own story; they come from the

different rivers where she has worked as a river guide or doing wetland restoration. Their textured surfaces gently contrast with the plants. Thoughtfully placed with plenty of space between, each is treated as a natural work of art. The result is harmonious serenity.

Now Jessica, Hans, and Gerry reap the rewards of their efforts. Instead of spending their limited time in the garden weeding, watering, or clipping, they can admire the view while relaxing in this peaceful place they have created.

The street and public sidewalk generate a fair amount of traffic, but the sizeable berm, planted with assorted grasses and drought-hardy perennials, shields their gathering spot. Earth is an effective sound barrier, and the berm noticeably reduces traffic noise. Rustling grasses, chirping birds, and humming honeybees further mask the roar of passing vehicles.

The plants are arranged in naturalistic irregular patterns. Occasional breaks in the foliage invite a pedestrian to glance into the garden and allow those in it to see who is passing. The trio deliberately included this permeability so "you could have the experience of the street," which might include exchanging a few words with a neighbor or welcoming a curious photographer into the garden.

Their screen of foliage stands all winter. In early spring, they cut down grasses and perennials just in time for spring's show, "a bright wash of beautiful blossoms" on the cherry and nectarine trees. Fruit trees are the only

A stone path leads from the public walkway past a hand-made metal privacy fence to a sitting area tucked against the house.

plants in the garden that get occasional feeding; Jessica will treat them with fish emulsion if they look stressed. No other manufactured supplements or chemicals are used in the garden.

The summer look is dominated by silvery green foliage of grasses—porcupine and elephant (varieties of *Miscanthus sinensis*), blue oat (*Helictotrichon sempervirens*), Idaho fescue (*Festuca idahoensis*), switch (*Panicum virgatum*), Mexican feather grass (*Nassella tenuissima*)—and herbs such as thyme, culinary sage, and oregano. A handful of easy-care perennials contrib-

ute splashes of color: purple coneflowers (*Echinacea* species), blazing star (*Liatris*), and yarrow (*Achillea*). Hardy ground covers including creeping sedum, ice plant (*Delosperma*), hen and chicks (*Sempervivum*), and brass buttons (*Leptinella*) form a living mulch under and between taller plants.

Autumn transforms this serene outdoor room to a blazing wonderland. Not only are the grasses showy—at their largest size, infused with warm colors, and sporting diverse plumy seed heads—but the woody plants paint the walls and ceiling bright gold with accents of vivid red.

Vines add interest in every season. Spring-blooming honeysuckle, a fragrant pollinator magnet, clothes the entire front wall. Large-flowered clematis vines add bold splashes of color through summer. Jessica trains pinot grigio and pinot noir grapes on the panels of the metal privacy fence, which these can-do gardeners welded

opposite In autumn, the Yoshino cherry tree sprinkles bright gold leaves over the berm and grasses.

A berm clothed in assorted grasses separates the street and sidewalk (at left, just out of the picture) from the private deck at right.

together using cold-rolled steel and farm utility fencing. For winter interest, after the grapevines have died back, she weaves cut grass stems through the fence giving a look similar to British roof thatching.

Wildlife visit the yard—not only seed-eating birds but also honeybees, who arrive early and stay all year. Hummingbirds and quail visit, and Jessica has spotted an occasional preying mantis cocoon.

Drip irrigation reduces the workload and water use. Two main irrigation stations each run lines to several aboveground heads, and each head has multiple lines running from it directly to the root zones of individual plants. Plants with larger root zones, including the trees, get several water lines. If a plant is removed, its water lines are also removed to discourage weeds. Watering only the desired plants is an effective strategy for reducing maintenance in dry climates.

Jessica adjusts the watering system depending on the weather. She waters twice a week during most of the growing season, three times in especially hot weeks. The drip system gives precise control over how much water plants get.

Well-adapted plants are allowed to spread naturally to places the irrigation system doesn't reach. Despite Boise's sparse 12 inches of annual precipitation, many plants will grow without supplemental water in the right microclimate. Yarrow, Mexican feather grass, purple coneflowers, Idaho fescue, California poppies (*Eschscholzia californica*), and big sagebrush (*Artemisia tridentata*) have self-sown, adding to the natural feel and continuity of the landscape.

Other maintenance is minimal. The Trex deck is a sturdy composite made from recycled plastic bags and bottles and wood scrap. They oil it annually. Jessica periodically edits the plants, removing some to make room for the broadening clumps of tall grasses, and gives the extras to neighbors.

Most of the tiny front yards on this block are lawnless gardens that stretch from the front door to the public sidewalk directly adjacent to the street. Each has an individual style, and their diversity is intriguing, as is the fact that when passing you cannot see any of these yards at one glance. But it is easy to see they are outdoor living spaces in which people thrive along with the plants.

Four-season fruit trees

Yoshino cherry is a true four-season gem; it offers beautiful fall foliage, striking winter bark, spring bloom, and an edible harvest. Try also:

- Tree forms of serviceberry (*Amelanchier*, zones 3–9) are tough and early flowering, with showy red-orange autumn foliage and delicious small pitless fruits you can eat or share with the birds.

- Apricots (*Prunus armeniaca*, zones 4–8) contribute fragrant flowers, edible fruits, and fall color, and they are extremely drought and heat tolerant.

- Wild plums (*Prunus americana*, zones 3–8) can be trained into picturesque small trees; left to their own devices, they will sucker to produce wildlife-sheltering hedgerows and copious fruit for jellies.

- In the shade of larger trees and buildings where other fruit trees flounder or rot, pawpaw (*Asimina triloba*, zones 5–9) creates a tasty understory with tropical-sized leaves and golden fall color.

Serviceberry fruit is delicious if you can beat the birds to it.

opposite Peeking through its grassy wall rewards pedestrians' curiosity with a tranquil yet tantalizing view of the inner garden.

A low-care deck surrounded by foliage, fences, and walls creates an intimate space in which to relax amid stones of special significance.

Association Approved

Orlando, Florida

New plants were given a layer of fresh topsoil, drip irrigation, and a topdressing of pine bark mulch.

Kurt Vigneau and Mary Hughes's crisply manicured Florida front yard has no lawn whatsoever. It all began five years ago, out at the curb, with a parking strip entirely filled by Asiatic jasmine (*Trachelospermum asiaticum*). This creeper's thick growth holds the soil and keeps weeds away. "It is really the iron horse in the yard," says Mary. They edge it about three times a year to keep it confined to its bed and trim it with a weed whip every spring. It's versatile, too, she notes. "You can whip it down to a lower height or let it grow and it will look like a low-growing hedge." The glossy green foliage suffered no noticeable decline when they capped off the sprinkler system for the parking strip; the only water it now receives falls from the sky.

Kurt and Mary used to have a large front lawn, but they became inspired to convert it to a no-mow landscape as they learned more about the benefits of native plants. "Native plants not only complete nature's food web but they look pretty darn nice too," Mary says, though she and Kurt are not strictly native plant gardeners. She explains their philosophy: "We did try to go with native plants whenever possible, but sometimes the right

The tidy front yard before its conversion to a lawnless garden.

plant in the right place will do a much better job. We need to be as flexible as nature is."

After doing some research and coming up with a lawnless design for their front yard, they approached their homeowners association (HOA) with a request. The couple filled out forms describing their plan. "We wanted to remove our St. Augustine lawn and replace it with flowering shrubs, ground cover, tall grasses, and small accent plants." The couple used the nine principles of Florida-friendly landscaping, which are mandated in a 2009 state law to combat environmental degradation resulting from overdevelopment throughout the state. After a visit with the director and president of the HOA, they received permission to implement their design.

Kurt and Mary did all of their lawn conversion work themselves. "Thank goodness we have a pickup truck," she chuckles. They dug out some existing shrubs, and they stripped off their turf with a garden fork. "St. Augus-

tine grass has very shallow roots," says Mary. "This is what makes this grass such a water and fertilizer hog." Turf and shrubs went to the local yard waste site, where they could be turned into compost for use by local residents.

As stripping the sod also removed topsoil, they spread three yards of premium topsoil over their new planting area to give the plants a good start. They made a point of purchasing all their plants from a local independent nursery, which sold the plants to them at wholesale prices because they bought so many. Kurt installed drip irrigation lines while Mary planted. Finally, the entire planted area was mulched with pine bark to give it a finished look and preserve soil health.

At the front edge of their yard, a swath of Asiatic jasmine swirling around a mature southern magnolia tree (*Magnolia grandiflora* 'Little Gem') was expanded to echo the parking strip. The sidewalk now passes through an unbroken sea of this low plant. Behind the newly planted

top An artistic combination of mixed shrubs, perennials, and ground covers now fills the front yard.

Mary Hughes and Kurt Vigneau are pioneering a Florida-friendly landscape in their neighborhood, and the neighbors are taking notice.

jasmine is a broad stripe of creeping juniper (*Juniperus conferta* 'Blue Pacific') and beyond that, a fringe of dwarf yaupon holly (*Ilex vomitoria* 'Schilling's Dwarf').

The holly's tiny leaves and sheared round forms make a tidy skirt hiding the legs of a taller mix of shrubs chosen to host birds and butterflies as well as for their beauty. Ruby fringe flower (*Loropetalum chinense* 'Ruby'), a nonnative relative of witch hazel, has

eye-catching red flowers and red-tinted foliage, making it a great substitute for pretty but invasive red-leaved Japanese barberry. A close-planted grove of native Walter's viburnum (*Viburnum obovatum*), which stays evergreen in mild winters and blooms in early spring, makes a densely branched nesting area with fruit for songbirds just outside the front windows.

Kurt and Mary's design considers humans as well as wildlife. Beside their front door they planted a native yellow anise tree (*Illicium parviflorum*) so its scented foliage perfumes their entry and wafts indoors through open windows. "It is root-beer-and-licorice scented. Really nice," she says. Alongside the front walk, a carpet of creeping bramble (*Rubus calycinoides*) spreads furry scalloped leaves and edible golden fruits. A living bouquet welcomes visitors where the front walk meets the driveway; orange and chartreuse wands of bulbine (*Bulbine frutescens* 'Hallmark') glow above sprays of purple blue-eyed grass (*Sisyrinchium angustifolium* 'Suwanee').

Across the driveway from the main part of the front yard, a narrow strip of remaining lawn was removed. They planted tall clumps of native fakahatchee grass (*Tripsacum dactyloides*) along the edge of the property, abutting the neighbor's St. Augustine lawn. Maintenance can be high at the line where two different garden areas meet, especially when one of the areas is lawn. Between their low-care planting and the neighbor's lawn, they spread a strip of landscape fabric covered with extra chunky pine bark. So far the lawn hasn't invaded, says Mary. "I would like to think that the native grass is scaring the bejeebers out of the St. Augustine grass."

The grassy hedge sets off a decorative mix of yellow bulbine, purple blue-eyed grass, and ruby fringe flower that mirrors the same combination across the driveway. Dwarf mondo grass dotted among the taller plants will eventually form a living mulch through the understory.

The couple "met just about everyone in the subdivision" while creating their no-mow front yard. How did these neighbors respond to their project? "They asked lots of questions, they got inspired," Mary says, "and they wanted to have 'the look' too!" She recalls working in her front yard soon after it was planted and getting a pleasant surprise. "I glanced down the street. There they were, a couple much like Kurt and myself, with the usual suspects in hand: a shovel, a rake, yard waste recycle bags. They were removing grass—not just some of the grass, *all* of the grass."

It took Kurt and Mary a year to complete their lawn conversion. One year after that, their new landscape has surpassed expectations. "Our front yard has exploded with growth," Mary marvels. "To our amazement, nothing has failed. Of course, having a septic system probably didn't hurt either." The septic field is located in the front yard below their new plants.

Mary reports that the HOA director and president have continued to be supportive. "When they do catch us outside they send accolades our way." The couple are reaping the rewards of their no-mow landscape. "Everything that we planted is extremely low maintenance," Mary says, "so much so that the folks that live in our subdivision now complain that they never see us." Kurt adds that he is thankful they made the switch from lawn to garden. "There are much, much better things to do with soil than trying to get grass to grow."

top In a narrow bed beside the driveway, tall native fakahatchee grasses add life and eliminate mowing.

Only two years old, this landscape will continue to improve every year.

Scented small trees / large shrubs

Yellow anise tree perfumes a garden room and brings nature indoors. Try also:

Garden coach and blogger Susan Harris recommends Korean spice viburnum: "It isn't the showiest of the bunch, even in bloom. But man, can it waft an aroma."

- Fringetree (*Chionanthus virginiana*, zones 3–9) may be a country girl, but she takes well to city life and is the center of attention at parties.

- Smaller Korean spice viburnum (*Viburnum carlesii*, zones 4–7) prefers the sidelines, contributing powerful fragrance from a shady corner.

- In hot, dry regions, fragrant ash (*Fraxinus cuspidata*, zones 5–9) can be shaped as a 12-foot small tree; casting very light shade, it's perfect for a small urban desert patio.

- A great alternative to banned invasive burning bush (*Euonymus alatus*), native witch-alder (*Fothergilla major*, zones 4–8) gives a one-two punch with showy sweet-scented bottlebrush flowers and blazing fall color.

Flow with Nature

Shoreview, Minnesota

Clouds of Joe Pye weed sway above spikes of blue lobelia in late summer, while foliage of sensitive fern and blue false indigo supply textural contrast.

Karen Eckman's home sits in the middle of her moderately sloping suburban property in Shoreview, Minnesota. Years ago, after her teenaged son awoke to 6 inches of water covering his basement bedroom floor, Karen installed expensive drain tiling and a sump pump. That resolved the basement flood problem, but she still worried that her home's foundation would be compromised by waterlogged soils.

She hired local landscapers Earth Wizards to reshape her land to shed water near the house without sending it off her property, where it might cause problems for neighbors and deliver contaminants and excess nutrients to a nearby lake. They designed and built a system of gardens covering roughly 300 square feet, designed to handle runoff from a 1¼ inch storm event. The gardens stretch from her side yard, where the runoff is captured, to her front curb, where it is infiltrated into roots and soil.

Karen's side yard was remade into a 40-foot dry creek bed filled with river rock. It captures runoff from part of the neighbor's roof and all of Karen's, along with some from both backyards. As water flows over the rocky

A newly created series of gardens captures runoff in a sloping suburban front yard.

opposite After several years, the garden is filled with a diverse mix of native grasses and flowers. During early summer, foliage dominates as the plants prepare for their colorful late-summer extravaganza.

surface, it slows and sediment settles out; then it enters the first of Karen's two rain gardens.

The upper rain garden hugs one side of the front yard. At one end of this garden, water flows through a gap in a retaining wall, dropping into the lower rain garden where more rocks break its fall. The lower rain garden runs along the front edge of the property, and any overflow from it spills into the street.

As the gardens were sited on clay soil compacted during construction, Earth Wizards replaced three feet of soil within each rain garden, using a combination of 70 percent sand and 30 percent compost to ensure that standing water would be absorbed within twenty-four hours.

Native shrubs and grasses line the banks of the dry creek bed. Deep, dense grass roots and structural shrub roots help the soil withstand erosion when runoff rushes in from a storm or during spring snowmelt. This is Karen's lowest-care garden area. Her main chore there is clearing away fallen leaves every autumn to keep them

from blocking the spring surge. She owns a leaf blower but has found it more effective to use a pooper scooper or to simply scoop leaves from the rocks with her hands. Over the years, she has moved some shorter spreading grasses away from the edges of the creek bed. They hang over and impede water flow, make it harder to clean, and look "a little too wild" for her taste.

The plants have transformed her side yard into a bird habitat, its proximity to the house making it ideal for indoor bird watching. Black chokeberry shrubs (*Photinia melanocarpa*) are early spring favorites of the birds. Their large, tough-skinned fruits hang on the branches all winter, says Karen, and by spring—when fruit is scarce—have softened enough to eat.

A tall, narrow highbush cranberry (*Viburnum trilobum*) attracts migrating birds with a glistening display of red berries in late fall. Under it spread colonies of snowberry (*Symphoricarpos albus*), which has proven rabbit resistant so far. Juncos visit in the winter to eat grass seeds and snowberries. "A bird will land on the end

of a branch and ride it to the ground like a cowboy, then hold it down with one foot to eat."

Red osier dogwoods (*Cornus sericea*) also grace the dry creek bed. Like many northern gardeners, Karen appreciates their contribution when color is scarce or nonexistent. "They are beautiful in winter, especially when the snow sticks in the crotches of their red branches."

The rain gardens include more than thirty plant species, most native, with different bloom times and heights for a diverse natural community. On the drier edges in sun, columbine (*Aquilegia canadensis*) and prairie smoke (*Geum triflorum*) contribute early flowers, and the fluffy white heads of gone-to-seed thimbleweed (*Anemone cylindrica*) supply materials for nesting goldfinches. Canada anemone (*Anemone canadensis*) runs through wetter places, tying together taller plants and boosting the garden's absorbency. Shade-adapted Pennsylvania sedge (*Carex pensylvanica*) spreads under it, stabilizing the steep bank of the lower rain garden.

These gardens are at their showiest in late summer, boasting pink clouds of Joe Pye weed (*Eutrochium purpureum*), cool spikes of blue lobelia (*Lobelia siphilitica*) and hoary vervain (*Verbena stricta*), and clustered magenta flower heads of swamp milkweed (*Asclepias incarnata*). During this season it is the boldly lobed foliage of sensitive fern (*Onoclea sensibilis*) that fills gaps between sparsely stemmed taller flowers. Nearby, thick patches of boneset (*Eupatorium perfoliatum*), blue false indigo (*Baptisia australis*), and black-eyed Susan (*Rudbeckia hirta*) leave little room for unwanted plants to gain a foothold.

Joe Pye weed's 7-foot-tall powder puffs make appealing winter sculptures. "They look like ancient plants," says Karen. They offer prime wildlife habitat too. Birds—especially goldfinches—gorge on their generous seed heads.

Between her lower rain garden and the curb, Karen included a narrow strip of lawn; this turf border makes the rain garden tidier and more attractive to neighbors.

However, despite the professional rubber edging she installed, some of the worst "weeds" are the turfgrasses that creep into the gardens.

Even her desirable native plants need periodic editing. (She uses no chemicals in her landscape, and manually digs or pulls unwanted plants.) "I'm the Nazi when it comes to that, and I learned it the hard way," she admits. She started out thinking she would let nature take its course in the gardens but soon realized that if she didn't intervene, a few plants would overwhelm their companions. She removed fringed brome grass (*Bromus ciliatus*) and obedient plant (*Physostegia virginiana*) altogether and pulls up running stems of Pennsylvania sedge and Canada anemone where they aren't wanted. She is keeping an eye on sensitive fern, which has proven to be an assertive spreader.

Her gardens range from areas of almost total shade to almost full sun. Combined with the range of dryness to wetness created by her rain gardens, this creates an embarrassment of microclimates. She has observed how a plant can behave differently in different situations, and that makes it challenging to try to manage this diverse garden.

"It's full of surprises" is how Karen puts it. But that variability—by turns frustrating and fascinating—is the heart of wild nature, and of gardens that succeed in rec-reating natural communities.

top On overcast days and at dusk, the white flowers of Canada anemone glow like fallen stars.

Milkweeds are the larval foods that enable the miraculous but imperiled migration of monarch butterflies; swamp milkweed grows best at the water's edge, in wet meadows and prairies, and in rain gardens.

Dense low spreaders with decorative foliage

Canada anemone fills an early summer gap in the parade of bloom through the seasons, even as it fills the shady floor of a rain garden. Try also:

- Beneath the fresh green, heart-shaped leaves of American ginger (*Asarum canadense*, zones 3–8), red-brown flowers are hidden treasures.

- Strawberry begonia (*Saxifraga stolonifera*, zones 6–9) twinkles in the gloom, with luscious variegation and dangling white flowers.

- North American native Allegheny spurge (*Pachysandra procumbens*, zones 4–10) grows low and slow, unlike its quick-spreading cousin Japanese pachysandra (*P. terminalis*).

Allegheny spurge is perfect for spreading a lush layer of foliage under and among tall-to-medium-height shrubs.

- Supporting frothy white spikes of early summer bloom, the deeply lobed foliage of native foamflower (*Tiarella cordifolia*, zones 4–9) wears a variety of hues and two-toned combinations.

Artful Jungle
Berkeley, California

Marcia Donahue's thirty-four-year-old garden rises like a small chunk of jungle from its relatively unwooded neighborhood. Among the trunks of the trees grow several large shrubs and bamboos, and under these a complex tapestry of shorter perennials and ground covers. Here and there an opening appears, giving a glimpse of the house or another part of the garden. The sheer variety of foliage and flower marks the home of a true plant lover.

Though she lives in a densely populated urban area, Marcia was determined to make her garden an urban sanctuary, a place where walls and fences are masked by growing things, where traffic noises are muted by trickling fountains. "I wanted a feeling of total embrace by the plants," she says.

The curved trunk of a snow gum (*Eucalyptus pauciflora* subsp. *niphophila*) might catch your eye first, a pale smooth focal point amid the jubilant textures and colors. Its ghostly form rises from dark green rosettes of stemmed succulents (*Aeonium undulatum*) that swirl among assorted rocks.

Across the sidewalk, the narrow parking strip boasts a thick-trunked cabbage tree (*Cordyline australis*), more than a century old and bristling with sword-shaped leaves. Though its palmlike silhouette evokes its tropical origin in the South Sea Islands, it is winter hardy to zone 9 and evergreen, with fragrant spring flowers. It echoes the spiky blue Mediterranean fan palm (*Chamaerops humilis* var. *cerifera*) nearby.

The graceful weeping Monterey cypress (*Cupressus macrocarpa* 'Saligna Aurea'), standing a few feet away in a curly little pile of licorice plant (*Helichrysum petiolatum* 'Limelight'), also makes a strong first impression. Despite its delicate-looking foliage, it tolerates salt and strong wind and is well adapted to this coastal location. Marcia had no idea how large this tree would grow—nor did the nursery—when she brought it home in its five-gallon pot. It soon soared up into the electric wires. The city crew came by once and gave it a "Prince Valiant" haircut that grew out in about three years, so once again it hangs clear down to the street like a shaggy golden wall, "blocking the progress of the city street sweeper," adds Marcia, "who just goes around it."

She is lucky to live in the city of Berkeley, which lauds trees as "one of our most cherished features" and has developed an aggressive plan for increasing tree cover throughout the city to make it more livable. In light of this goal, Marcia's tree- and shrub-filled garden must certainly be seen as a valuable asset. Less fortunate gardeners elsewhere can face city strictures, neighborhood

Marcia Donahue views her exuberant urban garden as a "huge and glorious tapestry" of plants.

association rules, enforced mowing, fines, and other barriers to growing anything other than turfgrass in their front yards.

A renowned artist as well as an avid gardener, Marcia has over the years expertly blended these two passions. Many of her sculptures mirror or incorporate organic shapes found in nature. She uses durable materials that allow her to bring her art pieces into her garden, which she opens to the public every Sunday afternoon. She doesn't worry that the smaller ones will be stolen or broken. People seem to respect and value this fantastical

landscape she has created. It could be they take pride in a local landmark, she ponders aloud, then pauses. "Or they could be thinking a witch lives here."

The real magic is that Marcia has managed to create such a lush and private oasis when her entire property—including the house—measures only 60 by 100 feet, and just one skinny planting bed separates her house from the public sidewalk. Naturally, she incorporated the parking strip for its "valuable square footage."

The strip's compacted clay soil required improving. She dug out some of the clay, loosened the rest, and

Straplike leaves create echoes in the foreground throughout the garden, and farther down the path, weeping cypress hangs a smooth, lightly lemon-scented curtain between pedestrians and the street.

opposite Plants fill every vertical layer; sheltered by a mix of taller bamboos and canopy trees, lower-growing angel's trumpet (*Brugmansia versicolor* 'Charles Grimaldi') blooms above variegated Cuban oregano (*Plectranthus*) at left, New Zealand flax, and variegated African lily (*Agapanthus*) at lower right.

added soil and compost before planting up a storm. For this area, she is careful to choose tough, resilient plants that "can take a little stepping or are spiky enough that people stay off."

In a region where water prices continue to rise and a limited supply may need to be diverted from irrigation to drinking water, her garden's small size means that Marcia can water by hand according to what the plants need. She tries to give each plant just enough water to keep it looking good. When choosing plants, she gives preference to waterwise specimens that will thrive in her climate, which is totally dry during the summers, though she admits she is always on the lookout for "new and titillating" plants and feels "really gloating" to be gardening in a mild climate with so many plant choices.

Through opening her garden to the public, as well as just spending time out in it, Marcia has met and conversed with many strangers over the years. "Gardening is a nice way to relate to all kinds of people," she says, unlike hobbies that are more exclusive or competitive. "The quality of the camaraderie is sweet and generous." Visiting gardeners tell her she has inspired them. "Seeing my garden helps them realize they can do anything they want," she chuckles. "My message is go ahead and try it."

opposite Marcia's ceramic sculptures form an integral part of her garden.

A pink-red New Zealand flax (*Phormium* 'Maori Sunrise') is one of Marcia Donahue's selections.

Pale-trunked trees

Pale-trunked snow gum makes a riveting focal point for a garden. Try also:

- The leaves of quaking aspen (*Populus tremuloides*, zones 1–6) murmur in the slightest breeze all summer, muting less pleasant urban noise.

- For hot, dry locations, try the white-barked desert olive (*Forestiera neomexicana*, zones 4–9), a small tree with glowing fall color, berries for birds, and flowers in very early spring.

- Muscled blue-gray trunks of native blue beech, also called American hornbeam (*Carpinus caroliniana*,

Growing lustily in dry and windy sites in northern regions, quaking aspens have pale bark with black markings and golden fall foliage.

zones 3–9), show well in the damp, shady locations it prefers.

- Chalky blue bark with pale pink–toned patches make the small southern native sun-lover Texas persimmon (*Diospyros texana*, zones 7–9) stand out.

PART TWO

Situations

Challenges to Address, Obstacles to Overcome

With their semi-public nature and the stresses they endure, curbside gardens pose unique challenges. It can be hot out there on the inferno strip. Maybe it's not hooked up to an irrigation system. There's a big tree or electrical box to work around, or the soil is pulverized.

Learn how other curbside gardeners have successfully handled these and other challenging situations. You can too! In the process, you can get more garden—and more from your garden.

A well-adapted curbside garden builds soil, filters and absorbs runoff, weathers drought, prevents erosion, and attracts humans and wildlife in all seasons.

Working with Trees

A mature catalpa dominates a corner lot in Boise, Idaho, offering fragrant flowers; shelter from sun, wind, and rain; sturdy branches for climbing; a two-story view of spectacular natural beauty; and copious fallen pods, flowers, and leaves.

Trees can be welcome features in a garden, providing relief from temperature extremes and creating more comfortable settings indoors and out. Mature tree canopies offer privacy and cloak the urban built environment in year-round natural scenery. They attract birds and butterflies into urban areas. On the other hand, trees can be resented for hogging nutrients and water to make the understory unplantable, dropping leaves and fruits for the gardener to clean up, harboring pesky squirrels, and threatening the roof with brittle branches.

What Trees Contribute

Trees generally benefit urban areas. They can prevent or resolve problems that would otherwise require engineered solutions, and they make urban life healthier for people.

The air around and under trees is healthier for people to breathe. Tree foliage traps dust and particulates emitted by vehicles. Shade reduces ozone formation, which is fueled by temperature. Adding shade trees to

opposite In Oaxaca City, Mexico, the breath of a palo verde (*Parkinsonia aculeata*) makes dry desert air more comfortable for people.

A northern mockingbird gorges on late fall berries of the showy native yaupon (*Ilex vomitoria*) in Austin, Texas.

parking lots reduces evaporation of gasoline and emissions from heated plastics in parked cars, both factors in urban smog. As part of their respiration, trees produce oxygen and absorb carbon dioxide that contributes to air pollution and climate change. The carbon they remove from the air is sequestered in their tissues until they die.

Urban heat islands drive up temperatures to unhealthy levels in densely populated areas, as dark-colored pavement and rooftops absorb and reradiate the sun's heat. This affects not only human health but also the longevity of buildings and other structures. Trees shade pavement, cooling it by as much as 40 degrees Fahrenheit at ground level, and also they transpire, generating water vapor that helps cool the area under their canopies. Neighborhoods with mature tree canopies are cooler by up to 10 degrees Fahrenheit than those devoid of mature trees.

Shading the walls of a building cools the interior more effectively than using blinds and other indoor window treatments. Tall shrubs and small trees shading the west wall of a building will block the most intense and heat-adding sun of late afternoon. Chosen well and placed properly, trees can reduce air conditioning demand by 30 percent.

In winter, trees can increase both indoor and outdoor comfort, lowering heating bills as they shelter homes and gardens from chilling winds. Evergreen trees on the north side of a home or landscape shield it from the drop in effective temperature caused by wind chill.

(Large evergreens also host owls, contributing night music and mouse population control to a neighborhood.) In northern latitudes, the bare branch networks of well-sited deciduous trees effectively slow wind while allowing low-angled winter sunlight through to warm a garden space or a home's interior.

A mature tree can absorb up to a hundred gallons of water in a single day, making it a valuable ally for soaking up urban runoff. As tree roots grow, they stabilize the soil around them, making it less prone to erosion. Their root systems aerate the soil, improving its ability to hold oxygen and water. This benefits not only the trees but also their entire living community of companion plants and soil organisms.

All trees, even those that are evergreen, drop leaves. Fallen leaves insulate the earth, protecting roots and soil life from temperature extremes, desiccation, and erosion. This insulating layer reduces frost heaves of shallow-rooted plants during freeze-thaw cycles, and it keeps soil from warming too quickly and plants from putting out frost-tender new growth too early in spring.

Manzanita (*Arctostaphylos densiflora* 'Howard McMinn') doesn't like root disturbance, but it can endure neglect and looks striking in every season.

As the leaves build up on the ground, they attract soil life under the surface. Worms, microbes, and other soil organisms feed on the fallen leaves, and the by-products of this decomposition become food for the tree and its companion plants. Together, an interconnected network of underground organisms creates a well-structured soil food web with the capacity to hold water and organic matter, and this web is what supports healthy plant life.

Trees attract birds and butterflies into urban areas. They provide critical habitat for urban wildlife and animals that are migrating through. Many native trees can support hundreds of other species, from bugs to birds to mammals. These organisms mainly go about their business unnoticed by humans, but they are part of the aboveground food web that supports the life we do notice, like the songbirds that visit to eat the bugs on a tree.

As well as breathing cleaner air, people gain mental and emotional benefits from nearby trees. Urban trees have been linked to lower crime, reduced stress, increased satisfaction with life, and refreshed ability to focus on mental tasks. They also block the sun's UV rays, making a desirable ceiling for outdoor play areas.

Even if your particular tree is a nuisance to you, it may be performing these services that benefit your neighbors, your neighborhood, and your city.

What Trees Need

Given all the services trees provide, it seems worthwhile to site them thoughtfully and keep them in the best possible health while minimizing inconvenience to the gardener or negative impacts to property.

Growing a healthy tree at curbside can be tricky if its root zone is limited. Trees with access to less ground than they need are at a great disadvantage and have a significantly shorter life expectancy than those that enjoy unrestricted root growth. Trees need ample root space, not only for access to enough water and nutrients but also to stabilize their aboveground structures against strong winds, heavy snow and ice, and other adverse conditions.

Large trees need more root space than small ones. If located too close to pavement, they may send roots into the thin layer of gravel under it or infiltrate underground utilities because the soil around them is looser. Decrease the likelihood of these scenarios by giving your tree well-aerated soil throughout its root zone, enough water and nutrients to sustain it, and a large enough volume of soil in which to grow.

Tree root systems, unhampered, usually extend at least twice as far as their aboveground canopy of branches. As a general rule, a large tree that will grow taller than 35 feet requires a minimum of 40 square feet of root zone. For strips of land 2 to 5 feet wide and isolated islands of soil smaller than 4 by 4 feet, choose small trees that will mature at less than 25 feet high. For strips of land 5 to 8 feet wide and islands 4 by 4 feet to 6 by 6 feet, choose medium-sized trees that will grow no larger than 35 feet high.

Soil depth matters, too, especially in a restricted root zone. Where a larger tree's root area is limited, soil throughout the entire area should ideally be 3 feet deep, well aerated, and freely draining. Some small-to-medium-sized trees can get by with a 2-foot depth of well-aerated soil throughout a smaller root zone.

Trees will be healthier if you minimize soil compaction. Where foot traffic across the root zone is expected or inevitable, consider installing metal grates, pavement, or other sturdy materials that take the brunt of weight, leaving soil beneath and around them undisturbed and uncompacted. Your tree might also benefit from targeted, nondamaging soil aeration to enable compacted soil to absorb more nutrients and water.

To extend the root zone for an existing tree, remove sections of pavement and replace them with planting beds, stepping-stones, or permeable pavement. This will also give the tree more stability to withstand wind and significant runoff. When planting in compacted soil, dig several trenches radiating out from the planting hole and backfill these with loosened soil to encourage large anchor roots to develop.

When designing a garden that will include new paved areas, investigate use of structural soil, an innovative substrate that allows compression while encouraging (and supplying space for) tree root development under the pavement.

You can also improve the soil within the tree's reach to give it access to more water and nutrients. This might involve replacing or amending soil (working carefully around the roots) to add organic matter. If your tree requires regular feeding, supply additional nutrients via natural materials such as leaf mold, mushroom compost, decomposed manure, or garden compost rather than using synthetic fertilizers, which can harm the soil food web. Retaining fallen leaves is an effective and low-work method for building soil under trees, and it can be easy on the tree as well as the gardener.

Another way to improve a tree's health is to stop trying to grow perfect turfgrass under it. Turfgrass tends to spread its roots thickly in the top few inches of soil, creating heavy competition with the tree and reducing available oxygen in the soil, which can stunt a tree's growth. Fertilizers and frequent watering lavished on a lawn may promote disease and quicker growth, generating branches that are more easily damaged in storms.

Replace the lawn under your street tree with a garden of understory plants. Well-chosen companion plants aid in stabilizing the ground under a tree, as well as making it easier to let fallen leaves accumulate. Fallen leaves that remain under your tree attract soil life and encourage a healthy soil food web that will actively and continuously improve soil structure, so it will have plenty of pores to hold water and nutrients.

Choose plants that naturally grow under trees; their roots will be sparser and more extensive than lawn roots, they will be better adapted to sharing resources with the tree, and they will thrive in the leaf litter under it. However, keep in mind that native woodland plants may require sheltered, shaded areas, so they may not be suited to growing near a road, exposed to exhaust, wind, road salt, and foot traffic. If your soil was displaced or compacted when your home was built or during a subsequent improvement project, it may no longer provide a suitable medium for native woodland plants. Also, if your tree is limbed up or located near an open stretch of pavement or garden, its understory may get more direct light than a woodland floor.

In these conditions, use companion plants that naturally grow in partly shaded areas that are exposed to wind, poorer soil, and/or stiff competition for resources—bluestar (*Amsonia* species), wild geranium (*Geranium* species), and barrenwort (*Epimedium* species) from maple woodlands; bearberry (*Arctostaphylos*

uva-ursi), wintergreen (*Gaultheria procumbens*), and pussytoes (*Antennaria* species) from pine barrens; wild quinine (*Parthenium integrifolium*), zigzag goldenrod (*Solidago flexicaulis*), and sideoats grama grass (*Bouteloua curtipendula*) from oak savannas; harebells (*Campanula rotundifolia*), columbine (*Aquilegia* species), and alumroot (*Heuchera* species) from rocky outcrops. Low shrubs for restricted root zones under street trees include creeping Oregon grape (*Mahonia repens*), fragrant sumac (*Rhus aromatica* 'Gro-Low'), slender deutzia (*Deutzia gracilis*), and northern bush honeysuckle (*Diervilla lonicera*). In more open sites, well-adapted curbside shrubs include buffalo juniper (*Juniperus sabina* 'Buffalo'), lowbush blueberry (*Vaccinium angustifolium*), dwarf witch-alder (*Fothergilla gardenii*), and Russian arborvitae (*Microbiota decussata*).

If yours is a native tree, you might consult a regional field guide to find the plants that naturally grow with that tree. Investigate those plants and also related plants as potential companions for your tree.

When considering an action that might damage any part of a tree from roots to branches, keep in mind that trees are not able to generate new tissue to heal injuries; they simply grow to seal off a wound. The larger the wound, the more energy this takes, and the more vitality it can sap from the tree. Garden carefully around existing trees to protect their large woody roots from damage. Consider eventual trunk diameter in addition to height and spread when choosing and siting the tree; place its trunk far enough from the road that snowplows and opened car doors don't scrape against it. When planting under power lines, make sure to choose a tree with a small enough mature size that it won't need to be topped or severely pruned, as these practices will compromise its health and drastically shorten its life span.

Adapted to dry, nutrient-poor soil and a range of light conditions, purple coneflower and purple-leaved coral bells grow well under street trees.

Working with Water

A certain amount of water falling on your property or flowing into it is a blessing. It is absorbed into the landscape without your noticing and finds its way eventually to the groundwater or a nearby water body. After the garden has absorbed its limit, though, the blessing becomes a burden. Excess water can cause erosion, aquatic pollution, and flooding on your property, in your neighborhood or town, and for people living downstream. In more and more parts of the world, too little water is the problem, and capturing precipitation becomes not just a gardening challenge but an economic necessity, with a major impact on quality of life.

Too Little Water

You may live in a region where rainfall alone does not provide enough water for your plants. You may be suffering through a temporary drought during which your plants need supplemental water. Even in a climate that receives plenty of precipitation, your yard may have dry microclimates caused by shallow soils, excessive drainage, roof overhangs, or other factors.

Whatever the cause of your lack of water, if plants are growing in a hard-to-access location, extra water for them means extra work and expense for you. For short-term situations, it might be easiest to manually water the plants as needed. However, if your plants will need ongoing irrigation, a more permanent approach may be better.

As water is a shared public resource, your irrigation options may be limited by your city. In drought-prone regions, a city may restrict the amount of irrigation water used, either by raising its water rates or by limiting the times and days during which homeowners are allowed to irrigate. These restrictions may apply to you even if you have a private well. Some cities prohibit landowners from adding permanent structures, including irrigation lines, within any publicly owned or easement areas; this may affect how you can landscape your hellstrip or parts of your front yard. Other cities may require that you pay a fee or post a bond if you want to add a permanent structure to these areas. In some fire-prone municipalities, landowners are required to maintain irrigated landscapes within a certain distance of any buildings, and this requirement may apply even in areas where the landowner is not allowed to install a permanent irrigation system. It is worth understanding the restrictions that apply to your property before designing (or redesigning) your landscape.

If you do want to irrigate, installing a "system" could be as easy as spreading a perforated hose across a planting bed and attaching your garden hose to it once in awhile. Make it more efficient by covering the drip hose

A dry-adapted boulevard blooms with life in Boise's high-desert climate.

with a layer of mulch to eliminate losses due to evaporation, which could account for half the water you use in a dry climate. Irrigation gets more expensive and complicated, though still within the realm of the determined do-it-yourselfer, if you opt for underground pipes, precision watering for each plant, and automated watering.

If you want to grow food in a dry climate, an irrigation system is a practical necessity for all but the smallest garden. Even in wetter areas, supplying edible plants with regular moisture delivered precisely through drip irrigation will cut your workload and dramatically increase your harvest. However, for landscapes other than vegetable gardens, vineyards, and orchards, an array of strategies can help you design away the need for supplemental water.

Improving your soil's ability to store water can help you get the most use out of water that comes into the garden, whether from a pipe or from the sky. Adding organic matter, making sure your soil is aerated, and covering bare ground with mulches and living mulches will help conserve soil moisture.

Vertical layering imposes multiple plants between the ground and the sun, keeping soil cooler and moister. The plants protect each other from drying winds, and they emit water vapor, which moistens the air and cools nearby plants. Vertical layering means more leaf surfaces to capture rain, slowing its fall and giving soil and plants more time to absorb it. Like irrigating in short bursts with pauses between, this slow delivery ensures maximum absorption of water while preserving oxygen levels in soil, and that promotes healthy plant growth.

Judiciously placed boulders create pockets of moisture that help plants better endure dry stretches. They block sun and wind, creating cooler, moister zones below them. When days are hot and nights are cool, sun-

At Desert Botanical Garden in Phoenix, a living mulch of wormwood (*Artemisia* 'Powis Castle') conveys a sense of lushness with very little or no supplemental water needed.

warmed boulders condense moisture from the cooler night air, trickling it down to the soil.

If you live in a dry climate, be aware that native dry-climate plants will often space themselves to reduce their competition for water, and planting them closer together than they grow naturally will increase their water needs.

As a long-term, low-care alternative to irrigating, try using better-adapted plants. Drought-tolerant plants and those adapted to your local climate may need no irrigation whatsoever, and in fact may suffer if you do water them in the dry season or give them more water than natural precipitation would supply.

Consider moving a plant from a place where it is not well suited to grow. Perhaps there is a better site on your property (or a friend's) where it will thrive without aid. Use microclimates or make them. Place plants that need more water in the low spots where it collects, or direct runoff to them from high spots or drain spouts.

Turfgrasses demand the bulk of water used to irrigate landscapes in times of drought and in dry regions. Lawns can struggle or go dormant in these situations even when given copious water. Converting part or all of your lawn to a more waterwise landscape can be one of the simplest ways to decrease water use, and it can also make your indoor and outdoor environments more comfortable and rewarding. If you want to keep your lawn (or a smaller patch of it), replace struggling traditional turfgrass with water-thrifty grass species, many of which will need less or no mowing and no fertilizing.

Too Much Water

In the past, urban yards were designed to quickly shed runoff into storm sewers. As urbanization and runoff have increased, that approach has had dramatic negative consequences, such as flooded storm sewers releasing untreated sewage directly into lakes and rivers during major rain events. Runoff carries pollutants and particulates (not to mention precious topsoil) to local lakes, rivers, and streams, eroding banks and causing siltation, nutrient overload, and cloudy water, all of which can be damaging or fatal to aquatic life. As runoff flows downstream, it merges with other runoff to cause bigger problems, flooding water bodies and the surrounding landscapes. By the time a river reaches the ocean, accumulated pollutants from runoff may create a dead zone where no fish can survive.

Flowing water gradually erodes cement and asphalt—not to mention building foundations—and freezing/thawing water can damage the structure of these materials. Water that pools on a hard surface may contain salts and other contaminants that will attack the surface. Preventing runoff saves money by increasing the life of paved roads and paths, and keeping pavement drier is also safer for pedestrians and vehicles. Keeping moisture out of building foundations and basements prevents structural damage and the formation of molds and mildews, as well as aesthetic damage to interior walls, plus damage to personal property.

In urban and many suburban areas, impervious surfaces—roofs and pavement—generate more runoff than their surroundings can absorb. The runoff comes from precipitation and also from snowmelt. Even in dry climates, occasional or seasonal strong rains can be "gully washers" that create problems unless your landscape can absorb them. Lawns generate runoff too. A lawn that is sparse, sloped even slightly, or dormant sheds much more precipitation than a healthy mixed planting would.

In contrast, woodlands, meadows, and other natural landscapes generally absorb all the water that falls on them. Soil acts like a filter, stripping away pollutants as water percolates through it. Some water is taken up by plants, some replenishes the groundwater, and some makes its way into surface water, seeping in from the surrounding soil rather than flowing down the banks, in the process contributing far fewer pollutants and maintaining a temperature that is healthier for aquatic life.

Increasing the absorption power of each individual property will create many small, absorbent pockets throughout an urban area, and this can significantly reduce or eliminate runoff and its negative consequences. To increase your property's capacity to soak up runoff, improve your soil's absorbency by aerating and adding organic matter.

Plants will also help your landscape hold more water. The wetter your climate or the steeper your slope, the more plants you will need. Give serious consideration to including woody plants—trees and shrubs—for their superior ability to take in a lot of water. Grasses can also be strong allies, with their deeply penetrating masses of fine roots.

On sloping ground, plants other than turf are best. Thick growers with tightly bunched stems will actively slow the water, physically intercepting it and also pulling it into their roots. Unlike lawns, which have their leaves cut periodically and experience a corresponding reduction in their ability to support root growth, perennials develop deep, thick root systems over time, so they are increasingly effective at absorbing runoff, preventing erosion, and sequestering carbon.

Another way to make your property more absorbent is to use permeable paving or ground cover plants in place of impermeable surfaces like paths, patios, parking areas, private roads, and driveways (not to mention roofs—installing a roof garden can help you keep the runoff out of the drain spouts altogether). These alternatives also reduce urban heat and dust, filter pollutants out of air and water, and capture atmospheric carbon.

You can reshape your property to slow and soak up more runoff, delivering any excess safely to your chosen overflow point. Different strategies include berming up the earth to divert water away from vulnerable areas, creating rain gardens and bioswales to help slow and spread water, and installing French drains for moving water quickly between two points or under pavement. On a slope, terracing will slow the flow for maximum absorption. Combine these techniques as needed, making sure any overflow from your property does not cause problems for the next person or place downslope.

opposite Where lawn would grow thin at best under mature trees and Florida azalea (*Rhododendron austrinum*), woodland native blue cohosh (*Caulophyllum thalictroides*) cloaks a slope in artful foliage while controlling erosion and runoff.

Sunken islands of chokeberry (*Photinia melanocarpa* 'Viking') underplanted with coral bells absorb some of the runoff created by impervious surfaces.

Working with Poor Soil

The soil at curbside may be contaminated, compacted, and nutrient poor. It may not even be proper soil but merely construction fill with turfgrass rolled out over it. Air pollutants from car and truck exhaust can deposit unhealthy concentrations of chemicals including heavy metals on adjacent land. Since a healthy garden starts with healthy soil, you'll likely want to replace or improve poor soil. However, in some situations you may choose to accommodate it with well-suited plants and design strategies.

Embracing Poor Soil

If you can find plants that will thrive in your site's less-than-ideal soil, they'll have less competition and you'll have fewer chores. Stop fertilizing and irrigating, and switch to plants that don't want pampering. You can end up with more diversity in a poor site, as fewer plants will grow aggressively enough to overtake their companions. Or you might choose one or two signature plants that succeed in the conditions of your site and spread them around to create a homogeneous and natural look.

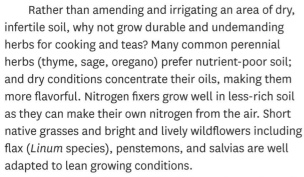

opposite A mass of potted succulents on a Berkeley planting strip makes an effective, texturally appealing garden.

Native to the dry, rocky slopes of California but winter hardy to zone 7, foothill penstemon (*Penstemon heterophyllus* 'Catherine de la Mare') doesn't need pampering.

right, bottom Nitrogen-fixing false indigo (*Baptisia* 'Purple Smoke') densely covers soil and improves its fertility.

Rather than amending and irrigating an area of dry, infertile soil, why not grow durable and undemanding herbs for cooking and teas? Many common perennial herbs (thyme, sage, oregano) prefer nutrient-poor soil; and dry conditions concentrate their oils, making them more flavorful. Nitrogen fixers grow well in less-rich soil as they can make their own nitrogen from the air. Short native grasses and bright and lively wildflowers including flax (*Linum* species), penstemons, and salvias are well adapted to lean growing conditions.

Clay soil, with its oscillation between too wet conditions and too dry, can nevertheless support certain well-adapted plants. Deep-rooted prairie grasses and flowers withstand these extremes. Some sturdy taprooted plants can break through compacted soil. Chronically wet soils, rocky soils, and every other soil type has its associated community of plants adapted to meet its challenges.

If your soil is so poor that improving or replacing an entire area is beyond your means, get creative with containers. It is easier and less costly to give a potted plant exactly the soil, drainage, and moisture it needs to thrive. Massed containers will require less fuss, promise quick results, and create a texturally interesting focal point to distract from any ground they don't cover. Use them to beautify a sheet-mulched area while you are waiting for the mulch to improve your soil.

There are even ways to get along with contaminated soil. If you cannot replace it, protect your kids by covering it with a dense layer of vegetation, a thick mulch, or hardscape, and grow your edibles elsewhere.

Improving Uncontaminated Soil

To improve soil before you plant, start by improving its structure. In small areas (or over time), compacted soil can be loosened manually with a fork or pitchfork, or by digging up clods and breaking them apart with a shovel, a time-honored method used by generations of successful gardeners.

Large or significantly compacted areas demand a sturdier tool. Rototilling will aerate soil but destroys the structure and compromises the soil life. The broadfork is a manual tool that uses the weight of your body; it can either loosen soil without disturbing its structure, or it can turn soil for double digging, depending on how you use it.

Milder, more directed approaches work best under trees, as you can work around roots to minimize damage. Try pushing a stick, stake, or other rigid object into the ground and then removing it to make holes at intervals throughout the entire area where water and organic matter can enter.

To quickly boost soil fertility, add dehydrated manure, leaf mold, mushroom compost, alfalfa pellets, or your own garden compost. In addition to adding nutrients, any of these materials will begin to build the soil life, and that will improve its fertility and productivity over time. In contrast, synthetic chemical fertilizers harm

Try bio-drilling compacted soil—planting radishes and other tough taprooted plants that will aerate it for you.

right Raised beds make it possible to grow healthy plants curbside without the back-breaking chore of changing out contaminated soil. They protect the garden from foot traffic and make harvesting easier too.

soil life and gradually degrade its structure, keeping plants dependent on future feedings.

If you have the time or are on a budget, you can enlist slower natural processes to improve your soil. Take a tip from savvy organic farmers and grow annuals for a year to build your soil. Cut them off at ground level in the fall and leave their roots to decompose in place; as they decay, the roots turn into nutrient-filled paths for water and new live roots. Plants with big, tough taproots can help you break up compacted soil as an alternative to digging. Let their roots rot in place to make channels of organic matter that will aerate and hold nutrients and water.

Another effective strategy is to sheet mulch (smother) the entire area for a season or longer. Pile on organic matter (leaves, grass clippings, chipped wood) to attract soil life, and those organisms will aerate and incorporate the organic matter into soil, decomposing it into food for your plants.

Improving Contaminated Soil

In our urban soils, toxic levels of lead are a common concern. This metal accumulated in many inner city soils from decades of vehicle emissions before leaded gas was phased out, as well as from some industrial emissions. Lead paint is another major source, and homes built before 1960 may be adding lead to the surrounding soil via weathering paint.

Letting children play in contaminated soil can expose them to lead poisoning and other ill health effects. If children will be playing in or near your curbside garden, or if you plan to eat plants you grow there, get the soil tested for common pollutants like lead, or simply replace it. If your site is contaminated with lead, motor oil, or other toxic substances, to ensure a healthy garden

you may wish to remove the top layer of soil (several inches for ornamentals, 12 to 18 if you'll be growing edibles, 24 to 36 for trees) and replace it with a good growing medium. An alternative is to add the fresh soil on top of your proposed garden, either contained in raised beds or mounded into berms.

When you don't need immediate results, selected plants and fungi can be used to clean up contaminated soils, a process called phyto- or mycoremediation. Particularly for larger properties, this can be more affordable than bringing in large machinery that may destroy soil structure, plants, and more in the process of decontaminating. Some species remove certain contaminants from soil and store them in their tissues; they will need to be disposed of in a safe way after they have finished their job. Others detoxify by breaking down contaminants, converting them to biologically harmless substances.

One promising plant for cleaning up lead in urban soil is the common annual sunflower (*Helianthus annuus*). Sunflowers remove lead from soil and store it in their tissues. When growing them for this purpose, boosting the plants' potassium level increases their effectiveness. After the growing season, cut the plants down and dispose of them like the hazardous waste that they are. Do not use them as compost because lead will be concentrated in their tissues. (This poses minimal threat to seed-eating birds, as it does not appear that lead and other toxins accumulate in the seeds to the same degree.)

While your sunflowers are at work, be sure to cover any bare soil under them with a thick mulch or a dense planting of ground covers to keep children and pets safer, since kids can be exposed to toxic levels of lead by touching contaminated soil and then putting their hands into their mouths. For an easy living mulch, sow seeds of Dutch white clover (*Trifolium repens*), annual sweet alyssum (*Lobularia maritima*), or johnny jump-ups (*Viola tricolor*).

Relying on biological processes to decontaminate soil requires more patience than removing and replacing it. For plants to clean the soil enough to grow food safely, or to purify contaminated groundwater so it is drinkable, can take a decade or much longer, depending on the situation. No easy, reliable information exists yet for the average gardener, but you may be able to find an experienced professional who has successfully used these methods. If you do experiment with using plants or fungi to remove contaminants, be sure to check your results by testing your soil before you allow it to be used for growing food or playing.

opposite If you can't do anything about your soil or the contamination is ongoing, cover it with a dense, low-growing evergreen shrub that children will not be tempted to play in; here, Russian arborvitae (*Microbiota decussata*) struts its winter garb.

'Teddy Bear' sunflower to the rescue!

Working with Laws and Covenants

Restrictive regulations may prevent you from designing the curbside garden you really want. You may find it necessary to compromise on your design in order to comply with height restrictions, prohibited plant lists, or other specifications. However, it is worth remembering that if your garden can challenge some of these norms and overcome objections, your neighborhood's or city's definition of what is beautiful might expand, making it easier for other gardeners to create less traditional landscapes too.

Know Your Regulations

Regulations may be based on public safety. For instance, municipalities often have specific codes governing street trees. Nut trees, fruit trees, and trees that are known to shed brittle branches may not be allowed on parking strips or next to public roads and sidewalks. A city may have developed a list of allowable street tree species, with all others being prohibited. In the narrowest parking strips, tree planting may be illegal due to concerns about root damage to pavement and general tree health.

Seventy-five percent of flowering plants as well as 35 percent of our global food supply (fruits, veggies, and seeds) depends on pollination by animals.

right Where city ordinance limits the height of her plantings on the corner, Minnesota gardener Susan Damon grows a low mix that includes blanket-flower (*Gaillardia ×grandiflora* 'Goblin'), wild petunia (*Ruellia humilis*), and blue grama grass (*Bouteloua gracilis*).

Check with your city or town before planting a street tree. You may find that if a tree is allowed in your location, the city will plant it for you.

Height restrictions protect public safety by preserving sight lines across intersections, around corners, or in areas heavily used by children. Site any structures with this in mind and choose plants that stay below the height limit, or be conscientious about trimming to keep them at a safe height.

In many neighborhoods and municipalities, regulations specifically prohibit native plants, food, or any other nonlawn landscape in the front yard, the parking strip, or anywhere in public view. Some of these older weed laws are being overturned as budget woes, water shortages, and shifting public opinion prompt municipalities to rethink their views about nonlawn landscapes.

A recent wave of challenges is coming from homeowners who want to grow some of their own food. (Sometimes the only sunny place happens to be in the front yard or on the boulevard.) Many curbside edible gardeners who have faced citations or complaints have succeeded in keeping their gardens and challenging the restrictive ordinances. Other gardeners, not so lucky, have been forced to pay fines and to endure negative publicity; some have had their gardens mowed or removed by the authorities.

When confronting a restrictive regulation, particularly one that was written decades ago, don't assume it cannot be easily revised or varied. A civil conversation, accompanied by a drawing or other description of your proposed garden, might be all it takes to convince the authorities to allow what you have in mind. In other cases, you may need to make a formal presentation to the board of your homeowners association (HOA), your city council, or another regulatory body.

You will stand a better chance of changing a regulation or being awarded a variance if you come to the bargaining table prepared to and willing to compromise. Take the time to listen and understand any concerns of the committee, regulators, your neighbors, or others involved. Address those concerns with facts, research results, and examples, and also by offering some alternative options. To assure that their concerns will continue to be addressed, offer to meet with them again after your new landscape is in place to discuss new concerns that may arise.

Working with them rather than against them may not be possible, but if it is, it gives you a better chance of success. However, maintaining a reasonable and conciliatory stance does not mean you must bow to authority that has no legal backing. In some states—including Colorado, Texas, California, Nevada, and Florida—laws prevent HOAs from prohibiting xeriscaping. Know your own applicable laws before you make your case.

If you can, get your neighbors to sign off on your plan (or express their approval) before presenting it to a governing body. This may defuse any objections on aesthetic grounds or worries that they will need to field neighbors' complaints.

Make Your Case with Facts and Figures

Though you may feel hurt or angry when your garden (or proposed garden) is threatened, try to leave emotion behind during dialogues with the authorities or skeptical neighbors. Your love of nature, your need for privacy, and your freedom of expression are important concerns, but they don't make convincing arguments if those you seek to convince do not share your values. Instead, focus on practical benefits of your design that are easier to quantify and communicate.

These benefits include services your curbside garden will provide. For example, your rain garden will reduce runoff over your property and neighborhood. Deep-rooted plants will control erosion on a vulnerable slope. Well-sited large trees will lower energy use for heating and cooling, saving money too. A hedgerow will shield you (and maybe your neighbors as well) from air pollution generated by a nearby road or industry. A buffer planting will keep polluted water out of a nearby lake, river, or stream by stabilizing the shoreline.

If your design will use less water than the lawn it replaces, that can be very convincing, even if the savings only accrue to you. Many municipalities face limited water supplies and infrastructure, so your using less does have an impact. If your redesigned landscape won't need mowing or blowing, that can be a savings in labor, fuel, and equipment for you; reduce air and noise pollution for your neighbors; and perhaps shrink the common area your association must maintain. Any way that you can assign a dollar figure to your garden will help—whether it's the value of services provided or the decreased cost.

Try to find ways to assess both the costs of your design and the value of ecological services it will deliver, and compare this with the costs of the lawn you are replacing. Often a nonlawn landscape will cost more than lawn to install but will save money over the long term, becoming more self-sustaining as the plants fill in, whereas a lawn needs the same level of maintenance and care every year of its life. Another factor in this equation is the economic value of the services the garden will provide, a value that will increase over time as the plants grow larger and more effective at filtering air, absorbing water, and otherwise improving their surroundings.

Visuals can help to make your case. Show photos from a book or from a garden that will help people visualize the kind of landscape you plan to create. Supply addresses so decision makers can visit similar yards for

Stripes of low aloe vera (*Aloe vera* 'Blue Elf') make an elegant edge between taller *Aeonium arboreum* 'Zwartkop' and pavement in a Malibu curbside garden.

above Tree health is one argument for converting the lawn under trees to islands of well-adapted, low-care ground covers like violets (*Viola canadensis*).

for you and your neighbors. It could even be a catalyst for citywide changes that dramatically cut costs, such as preventing the building of another municipal water treatment facility. You could end up a local hero, pioneering a better way!

Adding Appeal

Here are some design strategies that may address common concerns about tidiness and vermin:

Friendly barriers A border (sometimes legally called a setback) of lawn, low ground cover, or hardscape can make a wilder-looking garden more acceptable to those with traditional tastes. It can also keep the path or road clear of plants, ensuring safe passage and accessibility. Hardscape options for the border include crushed rock or gravel; stepping-stones, pavers, or bricks; or mortared pebbles. You can even make it decorative, using mosaic art or mixing materials to create patterns. Raised beds, retaining walls, and fences also work as tidy borders between garden space and pavement or public space.

Friendly plants Neighbors who are hesitant about lawn alternatives will likely prefer plantings that stay low enough to preserve the view, for maximum safety of cars and pedestrians. Unwanted spreading of plants may be another concern, so tidy mounds or neatly edged masses of plants may be most pleasing. Plants with large flowers have widespread appeal, especially if they are bright colored. Finally, plants that are familiar and loved may find better acceptance than unknown or unusual ones.

Lawn look-alikes No-mow lawns or ground covers that look lawnlike can save work and resources while preserving the look and feel of a lawn. They might appeal

themselves. This will not only familiarize them with the possibilities, it will also subtly make the point that others are doing this kind of landscaping, which can shift their view about what is normal and acceptable.

Taking the long and optimistic view, your property can model a new landscaping strategy. If your design delivers on its promises and looks appealing, you may see similar changes in nearby yards and public areas. Your yard will be a living example of a viable lawn alternative for authorities (or more cautious neighbors) to evaluate. It could prompt larger-scale changes in your neighborhood, bringing health benefits and cost savings to more traditional associations or neighbors who frown at the thought of a meadow, veggie garden, or other dramatic departure from lawn. Carefully chosen to fit the site, these alternatives can save significant water compared to traditional turfgrass, and they will not need to be fertilized or mowed as often, if at all.

Invitations for people Wildness puts some people off, though to others it embodies the very soul of the garden. To broaden the appeal of a wilder garden, include an obvious, generously proportioned path and perhaps a bench or other seating. For those not used to reading wild landscapes, these clear and familiar invitations inject recognizable order into the garden. Wider paths may alleviate fears about encounters with ticks, snakes, skin irritants, or allergens by giving pedestrians a choice about how much to interact with the garden.

Sponsorship by local gardeners Enlist a club or other local group (or form one) to care for a garden or to train maintenance staff. Garden clubs provide assurance that a garden will be well designed and receive ongoing informed care, which may be all it needs to gain approval.

Designed, installed, and scrupulously maintained by volunteers with support from the City of Shoreview, Minnesota, this runoff-reducing rain garden of native plants graces a local fire station.

Living with Vehicles

"You can see how busy our road is; I have to weed the outside edge of it on Sundays or else I am in danger of getting hit!" says designer Lauren Ogden of her Austin, Texas, hellstrip garden.

Roadways can deliver extra heat, dust, contaminants, and wind to curbside sites, not to mention unpleasant noises and fumes. Areas of your curbside garden might see occasional use from vehicles; this can include unexpected car traffic, planned guest parking, or occasional access.

Occasional Vehicle Access

On occasion, vehicles will inadvertently drive across a curbside garden. When your garden sustains accidental vehicle damage, there may be nothing to do but try to aerate the compacted soil, replant or replenish somehow, and let it go. Choosing easily replaceable plants for vulnerable areas will help you to fix and forget with minimal fuss.

Where bulldozers, school buses, and other large vehicles turn the corner too sharply and damage her hellstrip garden, Susan Damon fluffs the compacted soil with a small fork before patching any new gaps with extra plants from elsewhere in her garden. The transplants are watered a few times, then left to adapt to the harsh conditions of their new home.

A low but no-nonsense edge of brick protects plants alongside a brick-paved driveway.

right In northern regions with cooler summers, extra heat stored by sun-drenched pavement and released through the night can lengthen the growing season for edibles and their annual companions.

You might also prevent recurring damage by redesigning a vulnerable site. Would it be better protected by a low fence or wall, a row of plants or rocks? Could you use prickly plants or sturdy shrubs to discourage traffic, or brightly colored or taller plants to make the garden more visible to drivers? If the problem is ongoing, you may want to request that a cautionary sign or speed bump be added or a barrier to visibility be removed.

In areas that may see vehicle traffic, provide reinforced ground for wheels rather than letting them compact your soil, and limb up trees high enough to prevent damage to branches or cars. Your city may regulate branch height above roads.

You may want to use an area of the garden for occasional driving or parking. To design for this without giving up your garden, consider using plants that can be mowed when needed or installing a stretch of permeable pavement, gravel, or driving strips through a low ground

cover planting. Create a mowable or movable barrier if you want to block vehicle access to the area when you are not using it.

Heat Islands

Asphalt (or blacktop) absorbs significant sunlight, magnifying the heat radiated into nearby landscapes. A narrow strip of garden surrounded by asphalt roads and cement walkways will bake in direct sunlight at the height of summer. You can find plants that are unfazed by and even seem to relish these conditions. Heat tolerance is no problem for some tough plants that seem to take any amount of sun and heat they can get. In a sun-baked strip, spread a blanket of fuchsia-flowered annual verbena, silver-leaved gazania, or sulphur buckwheat (*Eriogonum umbellatum*), or delve into the wonders of your region's succulents and cacti.

Planting trees to shade both pavement and garden will help to moderate the soil temperature. As your trees become larger, they will shade more area and thus have a greater impact on their immediate surroundings. (Tree planting may be restricted or regulated in easements and streetside areas.)

Retaining soil moisture can counteract the effects of heat islands. Strategies discussed elsewhere in this book include growing taller plants and vertical layers of plants, shielding your garden from wind (though a breeze can also be cooling if it blows away trapped heat), using mulches and living mulches to cover bare soil, and placing boulders in plants' root zones to retain soil moisture. Exchanging some pavement for living carpets or organic mulches will cool ground temperatures too.

If you live in a cold climate or have plenty of shade elsewhere in your yard, a heat island can provide a

golden opportunity. Pavement lengthens the growing season for nearby plants and fosters a warmer microclimate in which you may be able to grow heat lovers that won't survive in other parts of your property.

Many edibles require a growing season that tests the limits of a cold climate. Peppers, tomatoes, squash, and melons depend on warm soil temperatures. A curbside garden that traps heat might allow you to grow fruits and vegetables that wouldn't otherwise reach ripeness in your location. Before growing edibles curbside, though, test your soil for contamination and give thought to protecting it from exhaust fumes, spilled oil, road salt, and other potential toxins.

Dustbreaks and Windbreaks

Old farmsteads used windbreak plantings of trees and shrubs to shelter their homes from chilling winter winds. Properly placed windbreaks reduce heating demand by up to 15 percent. Modern-day property owners might employ "dustbreak" plantings to shield their homes and gardens from noise, pollutants, and respiratory irritants generated by nearby roads.

Passing vehicles generate wind, and high-traffic roads and highways also bring noise and particulates from diesel emissions. Wind removes soil and protective leaf litters and mulches, and it dries out tissues of plants and tiny living creatures. Large or fragile leaves may be desiccated or torn. Small plants and soil life can be harmed and even killed.

A sturdy tapestry hedge of mixed shrubs blocks dust, wind, and noise year-round.

A protective dustbreak could take many forms: a row of trees and shrubs, or a fence, wall, hedge, or berm. Make it a four-season barrier. Even if your windows are shut during colder weather and your plants are dormant, do you really want airborne pollutants being deposited on your garden all winter? If you are growing edibles, this is a particular concern.

Permeable barriers such as hedges and trellises are the most effective at slowing and dispersing wind, while solid barriers—including paneled fences, walls, and berms—block wind but can create turbulence and wind tunnels in the process. In addition to slowing wind, blocking airborne pollutants and dust, and reducing traffic noise, a screen that includes foliage and roots can act as a barrier to excess lawn, garden, or agricultural chemicals that are applied nearby and brought into your property on the breeze or in runoff from melting snow or rainstorms.

If your gravel driveway or private road generates substantial dust, transform a problem into a solution. Replace it with a couple of paved driving strips through a planted area that can be maintained by occasional mowing. In addition to keeping dust out of the air, which is healthier for plants and people, this conversion will help to absorb runoff, cool the surrounding area, and make it more wildlife friendly.

Blocking Unpleasant Sounds and Smells

Plant foliage purifies the air. Increasing the amount of foliage in your garden can help counter strong smells from engines and nearby businesses and industries. Use pleasantly scented plants near your windows and seating areas—aromatic trees such as pine, balsam fir

Featuring assorted ferns and white-flowering strawberry begonia (*Saxifraga stolonifera*), a water garden covers the slope above Charlotte garden designer Jay Sifford's driveway, muting urban noise and freshening the air in his adjacent home and outdoor rooms.

(*Abies balsamea*), and basswood (*Tilia americana*); hedges of fragrant shrubs like mock orange (*Philadelphus* species), gardenia, spicebush (*Lindera benzoin*), and summersweet (*Clethra alnifolia*); and screens of fragrant vines including passionflower (*Passiflora* species) and poet's jasmine (*Jasminum officinale*). Place containers of narcissus, heliotrope, and other fragrant plants next to chairs, and lay carpets of aromatic ground covers beneath them. A fountain or mister freshens dry, dusty, or smoky air.

Berms make excellent noise barriers and are especially good at blocking low, throbbing engine sounds and bass notes from stereos. Solid fences are less effective

but still can mute barking, conversations, and children's shrieks.

It may be easier to add pleasant sounds than to hope to create silence. Nature boasts a diverse and seasonally changing palette of sounds. Use wind chimes, fountains or trickling water, rustling leaves and rattling seedpods, and the varied songs of animals that you invite in—birds, frogs, and insects—to mask less enjoyable noises. Give special thought to how you can create pleasant sounds in the morning or evening if that is when you use your garden most.

If you sleep with the windows open, consider nighttime sounds. Frogs turn up the volume in the dark. Many birds are active and verbal both morning and evening. Cicadas hum well past twilight. Geese on a pond or lake will gabble throughout the night. Find out which animal songsters are active at different seasons and times of day in your area and create habitat to invite them into your landscape. In this way, you can build a rich soundscape that will greatly expand your enjoyment of your garden.

Think also about noise, dust, and unpleasant fumes you might be adding to your environment. Is your radio someone else's headache? Is your leaf blower really more effective than a broom or rake? You may find silence makes your time outside more enjoyable, and your neighbors might appreciate it too.

Living with Wildlife

This roadrunner frequents the Albuquerque garden of Hunter and Barb Ten Broeck, eating lizards, small birds, and rodents.

Some animals perform services that benefit people, others offer hours of fascination to a human observer, and all are appreciated by nature lovers as part of the web of life. However, certain animal behaviors may threaten homes, gardens, or human health. Property owners can use various strategies to deal with unwanted animals, including barriers, distraction, compromise, and all-out killing. Desired animals can often be lured to live on a property by supplying their daily needs. Consider that your landscape design affects not only animals that live on your property but also those that move through it.

Discouraging Wildlife

You may be able to discourage unwanted wildlife by removing their habitat from your garden. Learn what they need in terms of food and shelter, and then eliminate it.

Rodents, for example, will be attracted to your garbage for its smell and to bird feeders for the seed that falls all around them. Removing those easy food sources can solve many a rodent problem. Geese prefer to dine on the fresh new blades of frequently mown lawn grasses

within view of a shore line. To keep them away from your water's edge lawn, add a 20-foot-wide buffer of tall plants between the lawn and the shore.

Mosquitoes require standing water or moist soil for a period of several days to breed. Remove places where water pools (including leaky outdoor faucets) and increase your garden's absorbency, and you will decrease your mosquito population. Mosquitoes prefer still air as their small bodies are easily blown about, so train a fan on your sitting area. (As a bonus, the fan's white noise will help to mask unpleasant sounds like nearby traffic.)

To keep populations of mosquitoes and other pest insects under control, consider inviting insect predators into your garden. Bats hunt down insects. Toads eat insects and slugs. Birds eat not only insects but also their larvae. Fish, frogs, and dragonflies eat mosquito larvae in water, and the last two also eat adult mosquitoes and other insects.

Amphibious garden helpers eat both mosquito larvae and the adult bugs.

right Urban predators play a crucial role in controlling populations of smaller animals that would otherwise multiply unchecked.

Rather than aiming to kill every mosquito in the area, you may find it easier and healthier to protect yourself. Try covering exposed skin with protective clothing, and experiment with essential plant oils (eucalyptus, wintergreen, peppermint, cedar, clove, cinnamon, catmint) that can repel mosquitos. This may only be necessary during morning and evening hours when the bugs are most active. Consider draping mosquito netting over your hammock or the umbrella above your outdoor dining table, setting up a screen tent, or screening in a section of your patio or deck.

Biodiversity will help to limit damage to your plants from leaf-eating bugs. Though some generalists can eat many different plants, most leaf eaters recognize only a few species as food, and some specialists are adapted to tolerate the individual chemistry of only a single species of plant. Mingle many different plants, making leaf eaters work harder (and expose themselves more to predators) to find their preferred food.

Humans don't tend to notice damage of leaves until it surpasses a certain threshold (around 10 percent). We don't tend to notice a particular kind of insect until its population surpasses a certain number of individuals. Rather than aiming to eliminate all leaf-eating bugs, aim to control their populations so that the damage isn't noticeable to you and so that the insect predators will remain in your landscape, controlling the populations of their prey.

Songbirds are avid eaters of bugs. Luring more birds to nest in your yard will have the most powerful effect, as they need a lot of protein-rich bugs to feed their babies.

In areas prone to ticks, make your paths wide enough to pass through without encountering foliage. Having other animals around can minimize your exposure. Some animals actively seek and eat ticks (pheasants, chickens, guinea fowl), while others will attract ticks and kill them while grooming (opossums, raccoons). Mice and deer, however, foster tick reproduction by tolerating higher levels of them on their own bodies.

While smaller creatures might spend an entire season (or their entire lifetime) in your yard, you have less influence over birds, mammals, and other animals with larger territories. Their regular path may lead them through your property, and they may grab a bite to eat on their way through, or they could choose to nest and raise a family there if conditions are more favorable than in your neighbor's yard.

Rodents and small mammals are prey species that require predators to keep their populations in bounds. Urban predators, though rarely seen, are more common than you might expect. Make room for these animals to coexist in your neighborhood, nearby parks and green spaces, and even your own property. Hawks, owls, weasels, foxes, and coyotes will be glad to take excess small mammals off your hands and your street.

As with leaf-eating insects, diverse planting can help limit the damage from larger plant eaters such as rabbits, deer, and birds. These animals are generalists but may focus on plants that are familiar foods to them, or a variety of plants may be nibbled but not decimated.

As a general rule, herbivores (plant eaters) are attracted to nitrogen content of foliage, to plants that are kept well watered, and to the milder taste and tender tissues of new growth. In other words, pampered plants are more appealing to them. If you cut down on watering and fertilizing, your plants may become no more interesting than the other plants in your yard or your neighborhood. If you add more plants, you will be less likely to notice when one is nibbled.

Try sharing part of your garden with browsers, and concentrate your efforts on keeping them out of selected areas. Plant clover, alfalfa, and other forage foods on your parking strip, and rabbits and deer might forsake (or never discover) the veggie garden inside your fence. Grow a mulberry tree, and the birds will abandon your other fruits when it is producing its delicious berries. Install raised beds or small fences around your flowers or veggies, while planting yummy weeds in the paths between them. A well-placed shrub out at the corner could have bunnies nesting there rather than under your deck. Piling the ripe seed heads of grasses and flowers alongside the alley could lure the mice away from your basement, and if they are living closer to the street, their populations can be better controlled by cats, cars, coyotes, and other predators.

Vertical gardens have the potential to take your edibles up out of browsers' reach. You can locate them against the house where they will be off the animals' customary path, and you can enclose them in fencing or mesh if necessary, as they are so compact. Other structures for protecting greens and other desirable edibles include cold frames, hoop houses, and greenhouses.

If you are really determined to avoid contact with particular local species (ticks, snakes, black widows, scorpions), maintaining an extremely tidy, barren landscape is a high-effort way to do so. Gaining more knowledge might help you find easier ways to avoid the animal and could give you more peace of mind. It may be that slight modifications could keep the animal out of your immediate environment. You may also discover you have been afraid of something that won't happen.

For example, porcupines are slow moving and don't actually throw their quills; you just need to keep your distance from them to avoid being poked. Wood ticks are easily spotted if you are wearing clothing of a solid, light color, and they can be pulled off and crushed with a small stone. Knowing that garter snakes eat mice and insects and are not venomous might help you see them in a new light, as garden helpers. Learning that bats eat bugs and that they navigate by radar so are very unlikely to crash into you might help you enjoy their squeaking and their soft wing beats as they feast on your mosquitoes.

While using poisons may seem to be the easiest and most effective solution to pest problems, it can create long-term problems that cost you and society. This is particularly true in a curbside garden. Poisons applied to small fragments of land such as hellstrips can easily drift into public areas or be washed into them by runoff, exposing those who pass through. People have varying levels of sensitivity to such chemicals, and children and pets are much more susceptible.

Non-target wild animals are susceptible too. Poisoning smaller animals (like mice) can be harmful and even fatal to larger animals (like owls) that eat them. Any broad-spectrum insecticide will kill a wide array of other helpful or neutral species in addition to the one you meant to kill.

For all these reasons, if you can find alternatives to poisons, use them. And if you must use a poison, never broadcast but only spot treat, consider applying it at night when most pollinators aren't active, warn neighbors and pedestrians they will be exposed, and make sure the drift stays on your own property.

Inviting Wildlife

Pay attention to what species are living in or passing through your area; you will have the greatest success directing your efforts to attracting them. For your desired animals, try to anticipate their needs for hunting, mating, and rearing a family, and for food, water, and shelter throughout the year.

Toads have long been hailed as the gardener's friend because of their voracious appetite for slugs and insects. They appreciate the occasional large rock or container plant, under which the ground will stay moist, and loose enough soil that they can hollow out a den there. An upside-down clay plant pot with a toad-sized doorway chipped out of the side works well too. Not the best climbers, toads might find their passage blocked by brick edging, curbs, or other smooth-sided barriers, something to consider if you would like to keep your garden toad-friendly.

If your curbside garden is cut off from the rest of the landscape by a stretch of pavement, the main wildlife you can attract to it will probably have wings. Butterflies, bees, moths, birds, hummingbirds, and dragonflies can easily incorporate fragments of garden into their territories.

Bees generally travel less than one-quarter mile during their lives. They need early-blooming sources of both pollen and nectar when they emerge in spring. Flowering shrubs including pussy willow and other willows (*Salix* species), bush cherry (*Prunus tomentosa*), cornelian cherry (*Cornus mas*), serviceberry (*Amelanchier* species), plum, and forsythia are early and abundant sources of pollen. Early spring bulbs such as low iris, species tulips, hyacinths, and crocus supply nectar at a time of year when it is very rare. This lures pollinators to live in your garden, so they will be at hand to increase your crops of fruits and veggies by pollinating them whenever they flower.

Note that the majority of our North American native bees are solitary, cavity-nesting species. Ground-nesting

Short native Washington hawthorn trees (*Crataegus phaenopyrum*) give winter birds what they need: juicy berries and a thorny haven from predators, be they falcons or urban cats.

bees dig holes in bare, dry soil and generally spend a year underground as egg or pupa before emerging to live for a few weeks as adult bees. Different species may nest in rotting branches and hollow stems of plants. Others live in abandoned mouse holes in tall grasses. Tilling, mowing, or mulching can damage their habitat and kill unformed bees.

For butterflies, hummingbirds, and other nectar lovers, provide flowers in different shapes and seasons, including flat clusters of tiny flowers preferred by butterflies and parasitic wasps; bilaterally symmetric flowers, which bees favor (along with those in the families Apiaceae and Lamiaceae); as well as tubular flowers for long-tongued hummingbirds.

Butterflies and moths commonly eat only one species or family of plants when in their larval stage. Larval foods are the limiting factor for many populations, so increasing the supply of larval food can directly and significantly improve that animal's chance of survival. For migrating butterflies, small patches of their larval food in roadsides, fields, and gardens can mean the difference between a butterfly laying eggs to produce another generation or dying without reproducing. Some butterflies overwinter in fallen leaves under plants, emerging early in spring. Cleaning up fallen leaves destroys the overwintering butterflies and cuts short that cycle.

Butterflies, fireflies, dragonflies, bees, walking sticks, and all other insects are killed by broad-spectrum insecticides and bug zappers, which do not discriminate between the useful or entertaining bugs, the neutral bugs, and the few species we consider to be pests.

One of the best ways to attract birds is to plant native plants, which they have evolved to use and will recognize as sources of food and nesting sites. These plants will also attract beetles, leafhoppers, sawflies, and other leaf eaters that birds prey on. Let fallen leaves accumulate beneath them; this leaf layer not only builds healthy soil but also harbors a diverse array of insects, supplying their predators (birds) with a reliable source of protein.

In addition to bugs, include a mixture of different plants to create a long-lasting buffet. Seed-bearing annual sunflowers, amaranth, and millet are popular with many songbirds, and perennial grasses and flowers will produce seeds too. Don't forget shrubs and trees (and some perennials) to provide berries in different seasons. Birds appreciate a bath, and the sound of moving water will lure them in as well.

Supplement other plants in the landscape—whether in your yard or a neighbor's—so you are offering food in a new season. It's especially important to think of late and early season foods. Fall berries are important fuel for migrating birds. Winter bird foods include seeds, late fruits that may not be palatable until freezing and thawing soften them up, as well as insect larvae and eggs that are deposited in dry plant stems or along living branches.

Give some thought to protection from predators and to the relative safety of your yard as a habitat for your desired wildlife. Urban free-roaming cats are responsible for killing many songbirds. If you are attracting birds to areas where they will be vulnerable to cats, help your birds stay safe by including prickly shrubs and thorned trees. These provide valuable cover from other

Floriferous native threadleaf coreopsis (*Coreopsis verticillata*, with the bright yellow flowers), waterwise and pollinator-friendly, adorns a lawnless urban front yard.

predators too (just keep those thorny branches out of your pathways).

If we intend to share our yards with other species, it is best not to apply indoor standards of cleanliness to the outdoors. Where you may see a messy area in need of tidying, birds will see a cache of food or nesting materials; different species use twigs, fibers of dried stems, mosses, lichens, spider webs, dried grasses, and even mud in constructing their homes.

Nature Corridors

Consider that your land may be part of an existing corridor (or could be managed so as to create or extend one) for wild animals that need to travel a certain distance to find food or a mate or to migrate. Corridors can profoundly affect survival rates, as each species needs a habitat of a certain minimum size to flourish. Animals can better regulate their populations if they have access to corridors; those that can't find food or that face stiff competition may be able to safely leave for another area where they aren't overgrazing or dying of starvation.

Plants also use corridors to keep their populations healthy. They can travel via wind, water, or animals along the corridor, mixing their genes with more, different individuals and establishing colonies in new locations.

Corridors are most important for long-lived species, which cannot adapt as quickly to changes in climate or landscape because they don't produce new generations as frequently. Unlike other conservation options,

A narrow roadside strip of land can be a resource-draining lawn, or it can be an oasis for wildlife.

corridors preserve not just individual species but also relationships and connections among different species.

You may have the power to interrupt or connect a nature corridor, depending on how you landscape your property. Notice where natural landscapes abut your land, and if possible, arrange your design to extend corridors to give plants and animals safer passage through more territory.

You may attract a wider variety of creatures if your curbside garden is part of a corridor that connects it to a larger habitat. Use the corridor as a way to share the land, letting animals pass through your property and inviting desirable species to linger. Keep unwanted animals moving by establishing a double hedge along the boundary. On the side facing the corridor, plant things they like to eat. This will lead them along the corridor. On the side facing your garden, plant things they tend to avoid, such as strongly scented herbs, prickly shrubs, or thickly growing clumps of grasses. The enticement of nearby food plants combined with the deterrent of a wall of unpleasant plants might just keep them from straying off the path to investigate your garden.

Shared fence lines or property borders can become effective corridors for animal and plant travel without impinging on human use of the property. Hard-to-mow ditches extending the length of the property alongside a road make ideal sites for linear rain gardens (bioswales) that not only add color and habitat but also do a better job of catching and absorbing runoff than when they are mowed. Effective corridors will typically be densely planted and as undisturbed as possible. The wider the corridor, the more species will be able and willing to use it.

A traveler refuels on Seattle's Pollinator Pathway.

Some states and cities are setting up corridors to help boost or support populations of different species. Seattle's Pollinator Pathway project aims to create a series of curbside gardens on residential planting strips, making a one-mile-long corridor between two pollinator-friendly public green spaces. The Wisconsin Department of Transportation has partnered with local gardeners to connect disparate habitats of the endangered Karner Blue butterfly. Farmers in Blue Earth, Minnesota, are being encouraged to create nature corridors or buffers along streams and irrigation canals as a way to add habitat, improve water quality, reduce erosion, diversify crops and income, and establish populations of pest predators to reduce reliance on insecticides. Instead of lawns or monocultures of nonnative species like crown vetch, Iowa's major highway roadsides are planted with native grasses, flowers, and clustered shrubs for runoff prevention, erosion control, reduced pesticides and mowing, wildlife habitat, and living snow fences; these beautiful roadside landscapes also act as corridors linking islands of habitat throughout the region.

Some of our best opportunities to provide nature corridors are the urban, suburban, and highway roadsides; undeveloped ravines; and waterways that bisect multiple properties. Often these places are not used by people, whereas they could mean the difference between other species thriving or becoming locally extinct. Maintaining them as lawns or groomed areas not only precludes their use by other species that genuinely need the territory but also wastes human labor and precious water even as it contributes pollutants from eroded soil, chemicals, and small engines. It is time to rethink this wasteful diversion of resources and to devote these spaces to preserving biodiversity and other valuable ecological services.

Living with Road Maintenance and Utilities

If you go to the trouble and expense of converting a public or semi-public location to a fertile, productive garden, you run the risk of it being damaged again (and again) by utility workers, vehicles, and equipment. Gardening curbside also means accommodating the by-products of road maintenance and working around equipment and easements located on your property.

Snow and Salt

In regions with winters of significant length, rural areas and suburban neighborhoods use snowplows to keep roads clear. Roads may also be sanded or salted. Most urban roads—perhaps sidewalks and driveways too—will be treated with an array of deicing salts. Depending on the particular products used, some plants tolerate this better than others.

Salts generally interfere with plants' ability to take up water and nutrients from the soil. They also stunt plants, disrupting their metabolism. Salt-tolerant plants have various genetic adaptations, including altered metabolic processes that let them absorb and excrete salts

to keep the proper balance. Plants native to deserts and coastal regions have generally adapted to living in saltier environments. These environments tend to be warmer zones; northern curbside gardeners may have fewer salt-tolerant plant choices.

To protect curbside plants from waterlogging and salt buildup, slope the ground toward the road or path. Even better, direct salt-laden runoff into a seasonal stream or rain garden planted with salt-resistant species. A berm, a row of salt-tolerant plants, or both can buffer sensitive plants from the source of salts. Whereas frequent, shallow watering will create a buildup of salts in the top layer of soil, deep watering helps to flush salts out of the soil.

Plants can also be damaged when snow is piled up by passing plows, by snow blowers, or by shoveling a walkway. Piled snow compacts soil and can delay plants' emergence in spring. Plants buried too long under melting snow can suffocate from a lack of oxygen in water-logged soil.

If you will be shoveling your walk or plowing your driveway in winter, make sure your garden plan includes an area for piling snow. As a paved area will generate runoff when the snow melts, a more effective (and beautiful) solution might be to create a rain garden or bioswale into which you can shovel snow or meltwater can flow.

Buried and Overhead Utilities

A quick call to your local utility company or state hotline can help you avoid gas lines, sewer and water pipes, and electrical cables as you develop your curbside garden. It's helpful to have your yard's utility lines marked during your design phase. Avoid introducing tough, deep masses of roots over shallowly buried utility lines; these are good places for elements that can be removed and replaced if necessary to accommodate utility work, such as paths of loose gravel, mulch, or stepping-stones; colonies of shallow-rooted ground covers; and annuals and other easily replaced plants.

Overhead power lines can be viewed as a ceiling under which you only plant trees that will stay below them when mature. Alternately, plan to prune a larger tree so it will grow around and above them. For this, choose a tree with limbs that grow solid and thick. Supple limbs that sway in the wind will be more prone to interfering with power lines. You can prune so all limbs are eventually above the lines, or you can winnow branches as the tree grows, choosing a few sturdy ones to be laddered under and above the lines. This treatment is much healthier for the tree than topping it, a practice that can be prevented in many cases by thoughtful choice of trees when planting.

Unsightly Equipment

Curbside gardens may house all manner of utilitarian but ugly structures, including signs, electrical boxes, fire hydrants, and telephone poles. Regulations may expressly prohibit attaching permanent fixtures such as

opposite Ninebark (*Physocarpus opulifolius*) soaks up spring meltwater and seasonal runoff, and can easily accommodate wet soil year-round, yet it also tolerates dry conditions once established.

Clematis climbs an elegant trellis, held to a signpost by wrapped wire and easily detached if necessary.

below Paperbark maple (*Acer griseum*)—a choice small tree for restricted spaces—decorates a Pacific Northwest streetscape.

decorative trellising to these objects or may forbid your adding stand-alone permanent fixtures to an easement area like a parking strip. On the other hand, if you use a removable fixture, someone (or a weather event) might remove it.

Vines are useful for screening unsightly objects. They can be grown on individual wires, metal fencing, sturdy latticework, or straight up a wooden telephone pole. Choose the right vine for the job by matching the vine's growth habit with a structure it can climb. Some vines (Virginia creeper, Boston ivy) have individual suction cups that help them cling to a flat surface such as a brick wall or a wooden telephone pole. Some (clematis) twine their stems around narrow wires, while others (hops) twine around a wider support such as a metal pole or wooden post. Vines that will grow a woody trunk (wisteria, trumpet vine) can hold themselves upright as they mature; simply prune back to the main trunk every year to keep them in check.

Match the vine's eventual size and growth rate to your location and your available time. Rapid growers may need trimming two or more times a year. For minimal maintenance, grow annual vines (including edible beans, tomatoes, and cucumbers) that die to the ground every autumn, or select perennial vines that have a limited height at maturity.

Wrap the base of a telephone pole or metal post with wire fencing if needed to get your vine started. You may need to keep this support in place permanently, but you can easily access the pole for maintenance by detaching your support structure and pulling it away from the pole along with the vine, then reattaching later.

Shrubs can conceal metal boxes and other equipment from view in most or all seasons. They also can be maintained at a desired height, unlike perennials, which die down for the winter (or are compressed gradually by snow) and then have to spend time growing tall enough to hide the box again every year. When using foliage to hide electrical boxes and other utility containers, remember to keep a clear access to any doors and allow their complete range of motion.

If you can't (or don't want to) mask an object, try shielding it from view at certain vantage points within your garden. A tall hedge alongside your deck can screen out a distant billboard or nearby balcony. Tall, airy flowers or feathery-headed grasses in front of your windows soften an unappealing streetscape. When choosing plants to repaint your view, think of characteristics to enliven the scene in every season: spring buds and stem color, winter berries and bark, and autumn leaf color in addition to summer blooms.

Distracting can work as well as screening. Perhaps you can incorporate equipment that must remain clearly visible—such as a stop sign or fire hydrant—into the garden by mimicking its color scheme. You might also try composing a riveting garden scene to divert attention from an uninspiring view.

Nobody will be paying attention to the red fire hydrant while this hibiscus is blooming.

Living with the Public

A densely populated neighborhood in New York City balances
pedestrian space with plants
that improve quality of life.

Owning public or semi-public land means that strangers, neighbors, vehicles, and animals can move through parts of your property, bringing with them an assorted mix of needs, impacts, risks, and rewards. Gardening curbside is about gracefully handling interactions between these visitors and your land, as well as preserving enough privacy that you feel comfortable spending time out in your garden.

Pedestrian Traffic

Pedestrians, wheelchairs and strollers, children, dogs, and perhaps even horses will use the public walkway or road to pass by or through your property. Your curbside garden will mean different things to each of them: pretty scenery, an invitation to explore, a place to poop, an obstacle course for a wide load or rickety wheels. Your job is to balance the demands of these visitors with your vision and resources as a gardener and property owner.

One challenge will be keeping traffic contained to places where you have planned for it to go and where it will not permanently damage your garden. Elements

that can encourage pedestrian traffic include mat-forming ground covers, level places, and paved, graveled, or mulched open areas. Elements that discourage traffic include protective fencing, uneven or sloping surfaces, and plants that are tall or look uncomfortable to touch.

Walkable ground covers are inviting, doubly so if they release a fragrance when stepped on, and creeping plants between the pavers connect you to the garden viscerally as you walk. Delight your visitors by using aromatic walkable plants such as chamomile, mint, and thyme. Walking over plants, we interact with the garden rather than just observing. Sensory stimulation captures our attention, pulls us into the present moment, and refreshes us emotionally and mentally.

To minimize damage from foot traffic, enlist self-repairing plants whose stems are capable of rerooting when they are broken and come into contact with the soil. Self-sowing plants can seed to fill in any bare spots created by claws scraping away the soil or by outright digging. Running plants can spread to fill gaps vegetatively. These plants will be working to repair damage to your garden before you even notice a problem.

Edges and hedges marking your planted areas may help guide pedestrians. Protect your nonwalkable plants with a variety of hardscape choices—low wrought iron fencing, hoops of willow or bamboo, logs, steel or plastic edging, a row of bricks or pavers, regularly spaced and similarly sized rocks or seashells. Plants can serve as borders, too, whether traditional clipped boxwood, a casual line of garden sage, or other shrubs, perennials, or annuals for your desired height and look.

However, dogs in pursuit of squirrels and children fleeing their parents may not heed such subtle signals. Berming or hollowing the planting areas while keeping

opposite A thick, low mass of slender deutzia (*Deutzia gracilis* 'Nikko') keeps pedestrians on the walkway in the parking lot of Longwood Gardens.

A mortared pebble mosaic by Portland artist Jeffrey Bale makes a permanent welcome mat.

your paths level can be a more effective strategy. Given a choice, adults and most dogs will choose routes across level ground. For a more reliable barrier to passage, try a dense planting of low, prickly, spreading shrubs such as prostrate yew or cotoneaster, or where you really mean it, prickly pear (*Opuntia*).

Where your visitors will be parking on the street, make sure they can exit their cars safely, and provide a clear path to your door. Your garden will be more welcoming if you include occasional paths across parking strips to help people reach the main walkway more easily from their cars. Straight, wide paths may be the most comfortable for visitors, but if you have the space, an additional meandering route through your curbside garden offers a taste of nature (and an opportunity to smell the roses, or whatever you've planted) as they stroll to your door.

Short, decorative paths add durable, affordable artistic flair. Built-in art is also less vulnerable to theft than more portable pieces. Mosaic creatively used can imbue a garden with character and a human touch that intrigues and invites. Where there is little snow cover in winter, this feature can be appreciated year-round.

If fire is a concern in your climate, choose your curbside plants with an eye toward their moisture content. Idling cars may emit occasional sparks that can set long dry grass ablaze. Consider using succulent edging plants or a border of rock or stepping-stones along the street to guard against this possibility. Keep dry leaves and pine needles from accumulating in beds adjacent to parking areas and in the street.

Just as you shovel or deice your walk to allow public access in winter, you may need to clear it of garden-generated debris in other seasons. Design your garden to incorporate these materials as much as possible, to lessen your workload and waste load. Set aside space for piled snow. Plant sturdy shrubs under which you can pile fallen leaves and flowers. Choose new plants with an eye to the debris they might produce and whether and how your garden could absorb it.

Fruit or nut trees may yield a surplus that others will value. Check for gleaning organizations in your community. These groups will pick your extra edibles, either for their own use or for charitable distribution. Just call them to register your tree(s). Your fallen fruit nuisance could provide strapped families with delicious home-baked pies throughout the winter.

Consider those living nearby and passing as you clear your walkway. It may be friendlier and kinder to choose a quiet broom or rake rather than assaulting pedestrians' ears and noses with a leaf blower. When operating a snow blower or leaf blower, make sure what you are blowing stays on your property rather than becoming someone else's problem.

When clearing your paths, think not only of people's feet but also of their faces. Keep branches, especially prickly ones, out of their way. Arching gooseberry stems, sharp holly leaves, and allergy-inducing, pollen-laden lilies catch on (or stain) people's clothing, strollers, and exposed skin, turning your otherwise inviting walkway into an obstacle course or hazard. If you live in an area that is prone to ticks, it may be only neighborly to keep taller vegetation far enough from the public walk that pedestrians won't brush against it.

If you receive frequent deliveries (or have frequent visitors carrying babies), take extra care to make your paths smooth and easy to negotiate without looking down, and wide enough to accommodate extended elbows. Similarly, if you expect many visitors with wheels, make sure to offer a wheel-friendly path from their car to your door.

Vandalism, Litter, and Liability

People may not have the best manners or show respect for the hard work you have put into your garden. Just as you might remove valuable objects from your car before leaving it to be serviced, you may wish to keep parts of

your garden that are open and accessible to the public free of tempting rarities and objects you can't afford to lose. Or you may choose to trust in human nature and accept the consequences.

Your frequent presence (or signs of it) can deter littering, vandalism, and other mischief making. Regular care signals a human presence, so a garden that looks well kept may discourage negative attention. This protection can extend to your home and neighboring properties as well.

Consider the safety of the more public parts of your garden. Poisonous plants, for instance, might be better kept within your private garden if you have curious neighbor children. A mulch of fist-sized rocks makes a perfect cache of weapons for kids of a certain age and disposition. Training your imagination on these scenarios can help you weigh the risks and liabilities.

Your prominently located curbside garden will have a disproportionate effect on other people's perceptions (and your own too). In disrepair or obviously neglected, it leaves a poor first impression. Well designed and healthy, it will enhance your property and your neighborhood.

Preserving Privacy

Adding some enclosure can increase a garden's usefulness and the gardener's pleasure in it. Individuals need different degrees of privacy, and one person's needs will vary. A landscape that gives you choices will increase

Despite their thorns, curbside raspberries have widespread appeal. Expect some grazing by pedestrians.

your comfort and entice you to spend more time in it.

A simple way to make this possible is to add a wall, fence, berm, or trellis. In a very narrow space, vines and espaliered woody plants add vertical screening that can be pruned to a desired width.

Hedges need more space and time but bring additional benefits. Expand the season and variety of fall color and perhaps add edible nuts (hazelnuts, walnuts, pine nuts) and berries (mulberries, serviceberries, blueberries) to your landscape with a tapestry hedge or hedgerow of mixed woody plants. Create a habitat hedge of native shrubs, luring your favorite wildlife to live in your garden.

For a solid year-round barrier, choose trees and shrubs that are evergreen (yew, boxwood, holly), deciduous with a dense branching habit (for example, *Viburnum trilobum* 'Bailey Compact', which will stay under 5 feet tall without pruning), or deciduous with a tendency to retain dead leaves through winter (beech, hornbeam).

Pay close attention to the mature size and growth rate of your screening plants so you can predict and guide their future shapes. Formal, classically elegant lines of long-lived woody plants entail some risk since if one plant dies, it may be difficult and costly to find a replacement of similar size. As insurance, you might purchase a few extras and grow them elsewhere on your property to fill eventual gaps if needed.

If you have the space, consider setting any barrier back far enough that you can plant a garden between it and the street. Flowers and foliage partly obscure a barrier, making a friendlier "welcome garden" on the street side, while behind it your hidden retreat offers a distinctly different outdoor experience.

Including windows or gaps in a solid barrier can make your garden feel more spacious from within, and

Outside the fence (and obscuring it), pink oleander and fig 'Sticky Fingers'; inside, only the gardener knows.

allowing an occasional glimpse into your garden makes it feel friendlier, and perhaps also safer, to those who pass. Try to locate these openings so that when a curious face isn't glancing through them, they frame a nice view of whatever you want to look at from within the garden— your neighbor's rose-covered arbor, the sugar maple on the corner, a distant barn or steeple.

A permeable barrier lets in light and breezes, and it gives a partial view between garden rooms or between the garden and the street or public walk. Picket fences, latticework, and walls of pierced concrete make sturdy permeable barriers. Certain plants also work well. Imagine seed heads of tall grasses glowing in the sun, glistening with droplets of rain, swaying in the slightest breeze, and partly obscuring cyclists and strollers who pass by your front sitting area. Bamboos also make beautiful, partly transparent outdoor curtains (though some can be invasive), as do airy flowers with sparse upper foliage, such as queen of the prairie (*Filipendula rubra*), Maximilian sunflower (*Helianthus maximiliani*), sunset hyssop (*Agastache rupestris*), and taller salvias.

Even a barrier that is low enough to allow viewing across it can increase your comfort. There will be a sense of remove from the bustle of the roadside, yet you can still people watch and even call out a greeting; you can see and be seen. A low row of lady's mantle (*Alchemilla* species) or lungwort (*Pulmonaria* species), or a wider mixed border of short plants, can suggest the boundary of an outdoor room.

Annual plants make great temporary screens. If you aren't sure about that fence, sample it for a year by planting a hedge of corn or sunflowers. Or redesign your garden using different walls every year, maybe even in different places.

A garden arch sets a clear boundary between public and private while inviting a glance through it in both directions.

Building Community

Exposure to nature has been shown to correlate with increased generosity and altruism, lowered cortisol levels, higher satisfaction, better cooperation and con- flict resolution, and improved problem solving. Nature enhances our senses, our positive emotions, and our thinking.

Your curbside garden may be ideally situated to spread joy and generate a sense of community. Design for this by including a bench for basking in view of the garden, fresh food that can be picked and eaten by any- one passing, a sunflower house or bed of pine cones in which children are welcome to play, a bowl of water for passing dogs, or another creative invitation to celebrate right here, right now.

Located next to public roads and walkways, curb- side gardens command attention. They inspire passing gardeners and property owners with real-life examples of plants, combinations, materials, and entire designs that can be replicated with some degree of success nearby. They beget other gardens.

To increase the number of curbside gardens in your area, try these strategies:

- Share your extra plants. A tried-and-true plant that grows well in your yard is less risky than an untried offering from a garden center. Cuttings, divisions, and envelopes of seed can prompt a neighbor to start or expand a garden. So can offers of help.

- Form a neighborhood garden club, and help each other create gardens and learn to care for them. Garden clubs offer a ready-made support group as well as a source of plants and ideas for novice gardeners. They also convey tacit approval for experimenting with lawn alternatives and less traditional yards.

- Develop a list of plants that local gardeners recommend for different situations.

- Establish a local contest. Award a sign for the best alley or boulevard garden, or distribute certificates to many recipients for contributing to neighborhood beautification.

- Give tours of your yard and describe the rewards of swapping your lawn for a garden.

- Persuade a local agency or organization to offer grants. Lack of money can prevent people from landscaping as they would like to. Grants guide property owners toward designs that will benefit their local area, with elements such as waterwise planting, habitat development, or runoff control to protect nearby water bodies.

- Lobby to change restrictive regulations such as weed laws that favor lawns over alternative (often more environmentally sound) forms of landscaping.

A convenient bench invites pedestrians to relax awhile alongside a public walk.

PART THREE

Creation

Solutions for Designing, Building, and Managing a Curbside Garden

Think of your curbside garden as a welcome sign for your property. Designed thoughtfully, it can also be an asset to your community. As you create and care for your garden, learn to respect your site's innate character and work with it, for a rewarding and healthy garden.

This section details solutions that are unique to curbside gardens, beyond general garden creation and care.

A ledge of stacked brick lifts annual heat-loving verbena (*Verbena lanai* 'Upright Magenta') closer to the sun and to the appreciative eye.

Choosing a Style

Choose your curbside garden's style not just on the basis of aesthetics. For a more satisfying outcome, also consider the functional contributions of—and the upkeep required by—different garden elements. Some styles are more complex, and artistic gardeners use them to create a certain mood. Others are simply planting patterns that give a distinctive visual character. Each of these options could be right for a certain part of your yard. Mix and match to make a garden that works for you.

Monocultures

Monocultures—entire areas filled with plants of one species—can be simple to maintain, one reason we like lawns so much. It's easy to spot plants that don't belong, helpful if you're a new gardener or simply new to your area and its plants. Well kept, a monoculture conveys formality, serenity, and elegance, but it can be quick to show neglect. Massed plants of one species make a more powerful color and texture statement than diverse mixtures. They also lure plant eaters with the promise of plentiful, easy food.

What to include—and what to avoid—in a curbside garden

Include:

- self-sowing plants
- self-repairing plants
- compact or columnar shrubs that fit entirely within the planting area
- living mulches to deter weeds and protect soil from erosion
- extra plants from your garden and your friends' gardens
- spreading plants, even indefinite spreaders if edging is robust
- roof garden plants
- one or more paths linking street to sidewalk

Avoid:

- potential weapons such as fist-sized rocks
- face-high branches in the walkway
- loose pieces that will float away in heavy rains
- expensive or rare plants
- heavy fruits or nuts hanging over the path
- sharp plants that snag passersby
- easily removable items you can't spare
- permanent structures that can't be removed for utility access
- foliage that obscures signs or other safety or utility equipment
- overexuberant vines

Foxglove islands emerge from a sweet-smelling sea of alyssum.

Monocultures work well in narrow beds and small spaces. Edged and given a definite shape, a monochromatic block of plant material makes a sculptural or architectural contribution to the landscape.

Some plants grow best as a monoculture; they spread densely and keep other plants out. Since they hold the ground against weeds, they are low-care choices where their spread can be contained: areas edged by curbs, or beds surrounded by lawn where regular mowing will keep them in bounds.

Islands in a Sea

You may already have a bed of islands—roses, asparagus, bearded iris, or peonies—in bare ground; just add a living mulch to save work and resources. Living mulches provide a protective layer, boosting soil life. More roots in the soil means your garden will soak up more runoff and block more weeds. If you choose a perennial or thickly self-sowing ground cover, it won't need regular replenishing like wood chips would.

Extend the season by choosing ground cover plants that peak at a different time of year than the islands do. (Different bloom times help pollinators too.) Pair plants that provide contrast, or echoes, or both. Choose a living mulch that won't rise up over the islands and submerge them.

Drifts

Drifts, or sizeable groups of one plant species, combine the easy care of monocultures with the ecological and aesthetic benefits of increased diversity. Boundaries between groups of plants can mean more work; choose plants that won't travel or will mingle without smothering their neighbors. Massed plants make bolder visual and olfactory statements than single plants. A few compatible species planted in drifts can fill a large area; repeat species throughout a garden room or landscape for continuity.

Drifts of black-eyed Susan (*Rudbeckia hirta*) and Japanese blood grass (*Imperata cylindrica*) enliven a restaurant parking lot.

opposite, left Heavy concrete urns on rock pillars accent a formal planted island within a circular drive in Carverville, Pennsylvania.

opposite, right A seeded meadow of blue flax (*Linum perenne*) and love-in-a-mist (*Nigella damascena*) enfolds occasional clusters of lamb's ear and yarrow in Rebecca Chesin's Minnesota front yard.

Formal Style

Formal gardens foster controlled environments that soothe and refresh. They may employ clearly defined edges, planted and paved areas in geometric shapes, and significant structural contribution from statuary, containers, and other man-made objects. Paths are generally straight, leading to obvious, visible destinations like the front door or a sitting area. Symmetry and proportion are used to create balance. Predictable patterns in living and nonliving elements encourage relaxation.

Because of their emphasis on hardscape and their structural arrangement of plants and other elements, formal gardens shine during winter, when landscapes that employ color without structure have nothing to offer. Removable structures are a smart investment for a formal garden located on an easement or right-of-way, as they can accommodate the occasional bout of utility work.

Naturalistic Style

Feeling artistic? Experiment with designing your own plant community. Combine plants that grow together naturally in prairies, meadows, woodlands, or wetlands. Consult a field guide, native plant enthusiast, ecological landscaper, or restorationist for help choosing a living community that fits your site. To integrate edibles, study permaculture.

Under tall trees, plant some shorter trees and different-sized shrubs in addition to a lower ground layer. Even where there are no trees, use vertical layering to fill all available niches. Use grasses in sun, sedges and ferns in shade, to weave a common thread through a plant community, filling bare spaces above and below ground while holding up slim-stalked flowers and contributing texture and other interest. Below them, add shorter perennials and ground covers.

Cottage Style

Cottage gardens radiate exuberant abundance. Owing to the limited space, time, and resources of their creators, they traditionally included flowers for cutting, edibles for eating, vines, and shrubs in a colorful hodgepodge, with very little room devoted to sitting areas or other open space. This style of garden is especially exciting for kids, and a great way for gardeners to increase their repertoire of plants.

Flowers, grasses, ground covers, shrubs, containers, and garden art mingle just outside the door.

Stroll Gardens

In a larger curbside area, a stroll garden designed around one or more paths will invite investigation. Echo plantings and other elements across the walkway or driveway to transform it into a garden path. Add auxiliary paths as space allows.

Lure explorers by using diversity of texture, form, color, light and shade, materials, styles, and topography. Screen and reveal views to add mystery and generate anticipation. Offer periodic rewards including artworks, fountains, aromatic plants, and other sensory treats, along with seating for the weary wanderer.

Urban Farms

Edibles can be incorporated into curbside gardens of any style, or they can be grown in separate beds like a miniature farm. It may be necessary to bring in soil to grow healthy food in a place that has been exposed to street-borne contaminants.

Pretty up a utilitarian veggie garden with decorative hardscaping. Alongside and among the edibles, include long-blooming annual companions like cosmos, marigolds, and zinnias. Aromatic herbs contribute leaf textures over a long season of interest. Low shrubs add focal points, winter structure, and shelters for bug-eating toads and birds.

Some edibles leave a bare spot once harvested. For a curbside garden on view all season, choose perennial veggies, fruits, and greens; harvest the leaves of annual greens rather than taking entire plants; and plant crops in succession—by staggering one crop over time or interplanting crops with different-length growing seasons—to prolong the harvest and the show.

opposite Even a familiar path can take you on a new journey each time you visit.

below Long-blooming pot marigold (*Calendula officinalis*) cheerfully outlines boulevard onions.

Choosing Plants

With its prominent buds over winter, faint perfume, and preference for the sunny side of a building, old-fashioned oriental paperbush (*Edgeworthia chrysantha*) is well sited near a window or door.

Countless plants flourish in any decent soil, and some will grow on even the most bedraggled or abused piece of land. Learn your site well enough to choose appropriate plants and help them thrive. Match the care they need to your available time and resources to keep your garden looking great long-term.

Friendly Plants

What makes a plant attractive or annoying varies by person. In general, we are drawn to plants that reward us with fragrances, textures, food, inspiration, and other pleasant experiences. We are more cautious around plants that cause us inconvenience or pose danger: those that are thorny or prickly, block our view or our exit, or are perceived as harboring ticks, snakes, or other animals we want to avoid.

Plants that invite touching engender good will. Add curbside appeal with furry foliage, airy plumes, and smooth, satiny leaves or bark. Charismatic but thorny plants like golden barrel cactus (*Echinocactus grusonii*) may still attract admiring glances and outstretched fingers with their highly textured surfaces.

above, left Who doesn't love a cherry tomato? 'Chocolate Cherry' is a visual feast.

above, right Touchable if you're cautious about it, leathery, two-toned *Agave americana* 'Mediopicta Alba' invites closer examination.

Ruffled satin petals and fuzzy buds of oriental poppy (*Papaver orientale* 'Harvest Moon') beg to be stroked.

Many plants feel great underfoot. Their textures, their coolness, and their variability create intriguing sensory experiences, even through the soles of shoes. Walkable mat formers include pussytoes (*Antennaria* species), golden creeping jenny (*Lysimachia nummularia* 'Aurea'), creeping forms of veronica, small-leaved creeping sedums, and silver carpet (*Dymondia margaretae*). Those that release aromas when trod upon include pennyroyal (*Mentha pulegium*), chamomile (*Chamaemelum nobile*), and prostrate thymes (forms of *Thymus*, available in a range of scents from lime to orange to pineapple).

Not all low growers are equally self-repairing. Stepping doesn't easily damage the flat gray-blue foliage of small-leaf pussytoes (*Antennaria parvifolia*), so designer Lauren Springer Ogden uses it to fill cracks between stepping-stones, but she plants crushable succulent ice plant (*Delosperma* 'Mesa Verde') alongside a path rather than in it.

to grow them even in unsuitable sites and regions for these connections. Our curious minds are also captivated by unusual flowers, different patterns and shapes of foliage, and rarely seen colors and forms.

While adults judge a garden primarily on visual appeal, children gauge its opportunities for play. Touchable plants are child-friendly, as are plants with "loose parts" that encourage imaginative games, such as detachable finger-puppet flowers of snapdragons, removable and replaceable joints of reeds, and sticky flowers of mountain laurel (*Kalmia* species) for instant earrings.

Children experience a place with their entire bodies; they are drawn to shrubs and weeping trees that create cavelike rooms for hiding and exploring, boulders and sturdy tree limbs for climbing. They seek interactions with plants and animals, and diversity excites them. Childhood memories forged in a garden bring joy and comfort throughout later life.

Replaceable and Self-Repairing Plants

Unless you can afford to lose them, rare or costly specimens have no place in a curbside garden. Use inexpensive or easily replaced plants, or those that can repair themselves.

Seedlings or divisions from an established garden are a cheap and easy source of plants. Seek plants that abound elsewhere on your property or in a friend or

Short plants weave a tapestry of color and texture that is visible at a glance, enhances a house rather than hiding it, and preserves sunlight for all. On the other hand, taller plants add movement—foliage bending and blowing, living creatures flitting to and fro at eye level—and they give more scope for creating a variety of experiences and moods. Tidy, mounding plants win affection for their aesthetically pleasing symmetry and predictable (thus easily controlled) growth. Bold leaves and flowers excite with their drama. Beloved familiar plants hold memories and conjure emotions, and we try

neighbor's garden, preferably in a site similar to your curbside location. Passing along favorite (or tried-and-true, or any) plants is part of the fun for most gardeners.

Easy-to-propagate plants are another low-budget source of material. Choose plants that will supply you with more plants: perennials that can be divided, shrubs that can be layered, bulbs that will naturalize and spread into colonies, and plants with easy-to-germinate seeds that can be collected and sown, either in flats on a windowsill or directly into the garden.

Plants that grow well from seed may be considered a curse in scrupulously maintained settings, but they are a real asset in sites prone to disturbance. Short-lived self-sowers seeded among more permanent plants will temporarily cover any bare ground, preventing unwanted volunteers. These gap fillers might die out over time as your permanent plants expand to fill the space, or they will move around if disturbed areas continue to open up.

It's possible and fun to include patches of short-lived, self-sowing plants that redesign your garden for you every year. Try annuals like moss rose (*Portulaca grandiflora*) and flower-of-an-hour (*Hibiscus trionum*), and short-lived perennials that germinate readily in disturbed sites, including cardinal flower (*Lobelia cardinalis*), feverfew (*Tanacetum parthenium*), forget-me-nots (*Myosotis* species), and lady's smock (*Cardamine pratensis*). To manage a site with self-sowers, increase germination by raking the ground around plants after their seeds fall, scattering ripe seed, or collecting the seed and storing it to scatter in spring. Mulch only with a light layer of compost or not at all. Curb self-sowing by mulching more thickly, planting living mulches in the understory, and clipping seed heads before they ripen.

In walkable areas and beside paths, enlist plants

that reroot from broken stems or root along stems that are pressed into soil; these grow thicker and self-repair as they are stepped on. Some examples are chocolate mint, creeping bramble (*Rubus calycinoides*), deadnettle (*Lamium* species), and sweet woodruff (*Galium odorata*). Carpet-forming sedums also reroot from broken pieces.

Taller, dense, running plants will recolonize bare spots to repair gaps and damage. They may be just the plants you want in a curbside garden, keeping up appearances without a lot of help or attention from you. Try the herbs lemon balm (*Melissa officinalis*) and bee balm (*Monarda didyma*); the low shrubs creeping Oregon grape (*Mahonia repens*) and creeping sand cherry (*Prunus bessyi* 'Pawnee Buttes'); or powerhouse perennials Chinese astilbe (*Astilbe chinensis*), prairie coreopsis (*Coreopsis palmata*), catmint (*Nepeta racemosa*), and prairie sage (*Artemisia ludoviciana*).

Narrow-bladed grasses and plants with tiny leaves will more quickly and easily regenerate foliage damaged by foot traffic, vehicles, strong winds, ice, or hail. Some larger-leaved perennials are also able to form new leaves

A Dallas median sports an unmowed stretch of Habiturf, a mix of native grasses, with fluttery seed heads of blue grama.

opposite Slowly suckering northern bush honeysuckle (*Diervilla lonicera*) fills a fragment of land between hedge and sidewalk in the Minneapolis area, holding it against weeds and foot traffic.

throughout the season. A gardener could hasten regeneration and remedy a disheveled appearance with a quick clipping.

Annuals are the ultimate replaceable plants, useful if inspiration just hasn't hit or you want a new garden every year. Cold-climate gardeners concerned about snow and sand piling up during winter, gardeners with seasonally waterlogged soil, growers of heavy-feeding plants, and monoculture enthusiasts wishing to avoid building up diseases or attracting browsers can avoid these worries by starting fresh every spring with annual plants. If you do choose this approach, guard your soil against erosion in the fallow season with a mulch of straw or leaves or an established winter cover crop.

Alternative Lawns

A low, open stretch of green foliage has broad appeal. However, traditional turfgrasses are poorly suited to entire regions, particularly those with summer-dry climates and those that receive less than an inch of rain per week through the growing season. Even if you live in a climate where lawns flourish in other locations, they may struggle in a hellstrip or shady front yard, on a steep slope, or in another curbside location that does not meet their needs.

For those who like the look of lawn, no-mow lawns provide a possible solution. Better choices for lawns that need minimal supplemental water, little or no fertilizer, and less or no mowing include low-growing dune sedge (*Carex pansa*) in coastal California; silver-toned sheep fescue (*Festuca ovina*) in cool, dry intermountain regions; fresh green shade-tolerant Pennsylvania sedge (*Carex pensylvanica*) or Appalachian sedge (*C. appalachia*) throughout eastern North America; mondo (*Ophiopogon planiscapus*), dwarf mondo (*O. japonicus* 'Nana'), or liriope in southern regions with hot, humid summers; buffalograss (*Bouteloua dactyloides*), blue grama (*Bouteloua gracilis*), or Habiturf (a blend of low-growing native grasses developed by researchers at the Lady Bird Johnson Wildflower Center in Austin, Texas) in the dry West and Southwest; and fine fescue blends (such as

No-Mow Lawn, developed by Neil Diboll of Prairie Nursery in Wisconsin) in cooler northern climates.

Though not as nature-friendly as a diverse plant community, a monoculture of perennials or shrubs has several additional advantages over lawn: it can eliminate weekly mowing or trimming, it can be well adapted to a site that doesn't support healthy turfgrass, and it can provide habitat for small creatures, including those that eat insects, slugs, and other pests.

Many a front yard sports a low-care and socially acceptable "lawn" of pachysandra, plumbago (*Cerastostigma plumbaginoides*), vinca, or perennial peanut (*Arachis glabrata*). Creeping juniper, heather (*Calluna vulgaris*), cliff green (*Paxistima canbyi*), and other low evergreen shrubs may not be walkable, but they make fewer demands on the environment and on the gardener while supplying a carpet of ever-present foliage.

Well-Adapted Plants

The best-adapted curbside plants won't need supplemental water, soil amendments, or protection from foot traffic to stay healthy. Doing the research or hiring a professional before you plant can save years of trial and error figuring out which plants will persist without pampering on your site. Of course, experimenting can be part of the fun and brings to light more potential plant choices.

It is especially important to choose trees and shrubs that suit their location, as they are long lived and become more costly to move with each passing year. Gauge the root space available as well as the aboveground area and notice any obstacles overhead that suggest a maximum mature height for woody plants.

Native plants support local wildlife and tolerate the vagaries of a local climate, though compacted soil, exposed conditions, and other realities of a developed site may not support that region's native plants. Some species are native to vast areas of the continent, but local populations (also called local genotypes) will have evolved to emerge at the appropriate time of year, bloom when local pollinators can use them, set seed when conditions favor it, and have other traits that although invisible to humans will help them thrive and contribute to their natural community.

Drought-tolerant plants have evolved specialized mechanisms for enduring low-water situations. Plants with small leaf surfaces don't lose water as rapidly as those with large leaves. Plants with waxy coatings on

their leaves can resist drying wind and heat. Fuzzy or hairy leaves not only conserve water but also condense morning dew and fog and use them as a water source. Light-colored leaves don't absorb as much heat as dark ones, so they can live with less water as well.

Other plants have evolved to tolerate waterlogged soils. Knobby knees of bald cypress (*Taxodium distichum*) grow up to absorb oxygen when the remainder of the root system is underwater without access to it. By the way, this ability to survive without oxygen also allows it to send slender feeder roots into compacted areas such as the substrate under roads, helping it to find nourishment even when growing in restricted spaces where other large trees would suffer.

Plants that tolerate fast-draining locations, acidic soils, salinity, and juglone (a root exudate of black walnut and related trees that hampers growth of certain plant species) all have their unique, ingenious adaptations that allow them to surmount challenging conditions. These adaptations are genetic, and for the most part outside the control of a home gardener. Though consistent

intervention—soil amendment, for instance—may keep a plant alive in a site that is not conducive to its growth, choosing plants fit for local conditions is an easier path to a healthier garden.

In a favorable site and without competition, even a modest grower could take over. However, some plants tend to spread from cultivated (controlled) areas to cause problems in wilder areas. For example, beautiful though it may be, Japanese barberry (*Berberis thunbergii*) in our home landscapes is spread by birds to wild areas, where it smothers diverse native ground-layer plants, destroying habitat for the animals that depend on them. Good substitutes in a garden include elderberry (*Sambucus* species), smokebush (*Cotinus* species), ninebark (*Physocarpus* species), northern bush honeysuckle (*Diervilla* species), or weigela (*Weigela* species), all of which are available in purple- or red-leaved forms.

Sadly, you cannot rely on your local nursery to stock only noninvasive plants or to educate its staff about which plants are invasive. Check the website of your state's department of natural resources for a list of your area's recognized invasive plants. Why not avoid them and the potential hassle and guilt when a bit more research will reveal equally suitable alternatives?

If you need sturdy, salt-resistant, walkable, or drought-tolerant plants, look around at which plants are succeeding in difficult areas near you. Though too few public streetscapes showcase imaginative design ideas that you want to bring into your home garden, they do offer living testimony of a plant's toughness or lack thereof. Also notice plants in healthy-looking older gardens. Seek out a local garden tour or join a garden club, and visit public gardens, especially those in your region. Other gardeners have a wealth of information and experience to share, and they are generally happy to do so.

Earthshaping

Berms and Rain Gardens

Slight berming creates better drainage, the key to growing healthy heathers (*Calluna vulgaris*) in rainy Seattle.

Depending on your site, you may want to dig a basin, mound up earth to create a berm, or both; these strategies are called earthshaping. Raising or lowering the floor of your garden can help block unwanted influences like runoff and noise, or direct resources of water and sunlight to where you want them. Diverse topography makes a more visually interesting garden, and it adds microclimates, letting you grow more diverse plants.

Berms

Berms can significantly quiet traffic noise within your home and garden. Earth is a more effective noise barrier than foliage or a fence. Your berm need not be taller than cars to have a noticeable impact, but it should be higher than the wheels for best results.

Build a large berm by making a gently sloped hill of subsoil, sand, or rock and packing it with heavy machinery before you add topsoil, mulch, seeds, or plants. For extra stability, first build a core of piled large rock or stacked cement blocks, then fill gaps with smaller rock and sand. A small berm can be built using excess soil

generated by another garden project, or stripped sod that is laid upside down and solarized or smothered to prevent it from resprouting.

Expect a berm to shrink by at least a third of its total size over the first few years. Packing with heavy machinery will minimize shrinkage. If you can't fit a machine into your garden or would prefer a manual method, locate a rolling drum you can fill with water and pull by a handle. Surprisingly effective, these are also useful for packing newly topped-up gravel paths and driveways.

Mulch your new berm well or thickly sow seeds of a living mulch to limit erosion while the plants are filling in.

Berms improve drainage. In a dry, sunny site, you'll be able to choose from a wide array of succulents, Mediterranean herbs, and dry-adapted flowers and grasses. In wetter and shadier locations, woodland plants will appreciate the combination of regular moisture and good drainage. Soil-stabilizing roots of running shrubs will hold the sides of the berm against erosion. Good candidates: snowberry (*Symphoricarpos* species), sumac (*Rhus* species), and creeping forms of *Arctostaphylos*, *Vaccinium*, and *Cotoneaster*.

While a gentle berm may be hardly noticeable to others, a significant one may require a permitting process or be otherwise regulated or prohibited. Check with your city planning department before you get too far in your design.

A berm clothed in trees, shrubs, and evergreen ground covers creates a secluded front yard and a serene view from indoors.

Rain Gardens, Bioswales, and Seasonal Streams

Even in dry climates, runoff from pavement and roofs is too often viewed as waste rather than a resource. Many front yards still deliver runoff into the street to be carried "away" by storm sewers. A rain garden can intercept the flow and absorb some of it, reducing the burden on downstream neighbors and water bodies while adding an absorbent pocket of life and beauty to the neighborhood.

To choose an effective location for a rain garden, go outside while it is raining and watch where the water flows. Put the garden directly in its path.

Dig a level basin and pile the excess soil around the downslope edge. It need not be deep; a shallow, flat-bottomed basin can absorb a surprising amount of water if the bottom is made from a layer of well-draining sandy or gravel-amended soil. (You may need to replace or amend heavy, compacted soil inside the basin.)

Make it level across the bottom rather than bowl shaped; this will spread out water, slow it down, and encourage it to soak more quickly into soil. To slow it even more, break up its flow using impediments such as rocks, plants with thickly bunched stems, and mini-berm islands. Piled stones at the entry point will guard against erosion.

Rain gardens are generally designed to hold water for a day or two at most. Make sure your soil is sufficiently well draining and include an overflow in your design, a slightly lower point in the downslope edge that offers the water a clear exit. Like good insurance, you may never need it, but if you do, you will be glad you planned for it.

More effective for larger volumes of water, bioswales and seasonal streams are linear rain gardens that use the same methods to slow and absorb runoff into soil and roots, while directing it through your property to an exit point of your choosing. When the water exits the garden, it is diminished in volume and speed, so it causes fewer problems for the next property it enters.

To move water quickly across an area or underneath a section of pavement, use a French drain. Many styles exist, from curlicued metal grates over a ditch or pipe to skinny, shallow, open channels lined with tiles or mortared pebbles. Design these to include patterns and mosaics for added charm.

Rain gardens, bioswales, and seasonal streams create a variety of microclimates; use plants that prefer good drainage around the edges, and moisture-loving or flood-tolerant plants in the center where they will have access to the most water and will also be most effective at absorbing it. Pack plants together to fill the soil with roots. Include self-sowers, running plants, and bulbs that naturalize to fill spaces under and among taller plants; this will give you good coverage both above and below

ground and maximize the absorbency of your rain garden.

Don't be afraid to use tall plants. Just as berms bring diminutive plants up to eye level, swales and hollows sink statuesque plants so you can look their flowers in the eye. Grasses, with their thick, fibrous roots, are extra absorbent. Also include woody plants if possible. Their ever-present structures mean that woody plants will soak up water whenever the soil temperature is warm enough for active growth. In contrast, herbaceous plants must emerge from dormancy and build their aboveground structures, gradually increasing their capacity to absorb water as they grow.

Many people prefer a border of low-growing plants or lawn between taller plants and a curb. If you aren't maintaining an adjacent lawn, it may be less work to use a tidy no-mow border of shorter plants or ground covers rather than a strip of lawn around the outer edges of the rain garden.

left A slight depression next to the sidewalk intercepts additional runoff, directing it toward the thirsty roots of variegated Japanese sedge (*Carex morrowii* 'Variegata').

Black elderberry (*Sambucus nigra* f. *porphyrophylla* 'Eva') makes a riveting focal point for a rain garden or shoreline, while soaking up extra runoff more effectively than smaller herbaceous plants can.

Partnering with Nature

Earth-Friendly Strategies to Reduce Your Workload

In Southern California, an alternative lawn of blue chalk fingers (*Senecio madraliscae*) embraces its regional climate and aesthetic.

Our modern lives seem to be chronically short of time. Even if you adore gardening, you may wish to design away unfulfilling chores in order to spend more pleasurable moments in your garden. Your design, your plants, your climate, and your standard of tidiness go a long way toward determining your garden's maintenance requirements. You can design and build a garden to minimize ongoing care by preparing the soil well, using well-adapted plants, protecting soil from erosion and desiccation, and taking into account the movement of water, wind, and sun through your site.

Watering Wisely

A waterwise landscape will pay off as water rates continue to increase, and it can be surprisingly achievable. You may think nothing will grow in your curbside environment without being watered, but certain plants have adapted to low-water situations or seasonal dryness. Look for regional growers who specialize in plants for your climate. Investigate plants native to your region and to regions with similar climates. Plants currently

self-sowing outside nearby irrigated areas are also possible candidates. A little research will uncover more possibilities than you could ever hope to try.

If you must irrigate, water only those plants that need it. Set up irrigation zones, grouping plants that require frequent, regular water (usually vegetable gardens, lawns, and container plants). Locate these near a water source to make it easier to meet their needs. Farther from the source and in areas you visit less often, establish self-sufficient zones of plants that live without irrigation. You may need to water these plants while they are getting established.

When watering, do it thoroughly and infrequently to maximize deep root growth and drought resistance. Most important, deliver water at a slow enough rate that roots and soil can absorb it. Instead of saturating the soil, which robs it of oxygen, water for periods of a few minutes separated by pauses of ten to twenty minutes. Imagine trying to gulp down a gallon of water as it is poured into your mouth. Most of us couldn't do it, and we'd have water running down our necks. Plants have a rate at which they can absorb water, and if too much water comes at them too fast, they simply cannot use the excess. Delivering water at a slower rate ensures that more of it will actually be used by your plants.

Choose an effective delivery system. Sprinklers are old technology; they may be simple to set up, they may be cheap, and they may be fun to run through, but in many situations they are decidedly inferior at the job

A dramatic 800-foot drip-irrigated gravel garden at Idaho Botanical Garden showcases dry-adapted plants including sunset hyssop (*Agastache rupestris*), purple coneflower, blazing star (*Liatris*), Rocky Mountain penstemon (*Penstemon strictus*), and pineleaf penstemon (*P. pinifolius*).

Partridge feather (*Tanacetum densum*), bloody cranesbill (*Geranium sanguineum*), and blue fescue (*Festuca glauca*) don't need much water once they are established, but a durable soaker hose remains in the planting area for occasional irrigation in times of drought.

of delivering water to your plants. In relatively humid climates and in sites shielded from wind, sprinklers can deliver water efficiently to taller masses of plants and densely planted landscapes. However, in exposed areas, areas with intense sunlight, and dry climates in general, up to half of the water they emit evaporates before it reaches the plants.

Drip irrigation is easy and affordable, and it delivers water with little or no loss from evaporation, at a slow enough rate that plants and soil can absorb it. It minimizes water waste while preserving soil oxygen levels and promoting healthy plant growth.

One of the simplest irrigation systems uses soaker hoses made of recycled rubber tires and perforated to let water out slowly all along their length. Several can be strung together, and they are the same diameter as regular garden hoses. They are sturdy enough to withstand some stepping and do not clog easily, even with unfiltered water from a well or irrigation ditch. They also make easily removable solutions for easements and publicly owned areas where more permanent irrigation systems are not

allowed. After you have planted or sown seed (or both), simply lay soaker hoses on top of your curbside garden. An inch or two of mulch will hide them from view and prevent evaporation and degradation of the rubber. Leave one end sticking out of the mulch in a convenient location; to irrigate, connect a regular garden hose to it.

Drip tape has similar benefits and uses. It is not quite as sturdy as drip hoses (it can be damaged by shovels, for instance) but is flat and unrolls straighter, making it easier to work with in crop rows or linear beds. To keep it from clogging, periodically send water through it at a higher volume to flush it of debris.

Sprinklers, soaker hoses, and drip tape all irrigate an entire planting area. This means that when plants are added, moved, or removed, irrigation lines need not be relaid or adjusted. However, in sparsely planted areas and dry climates, these methods create work for the gardener because they water bare spaces between plants, which encourages weeds.

For very precise delivery of water, set up a system of short, small-diameter, unperforated lines tipped with

emitters. Water only comes out of the emitters, which are placed directly in plants' root zones. Place an aboveground head in each area to be irrigated, then attach multiple lines to each head. Your water source can supply the heads via underground lines.

Do-it-yourselfers can dig trenches to lay underground irrigation lines. Where the route passes through a tree's root zone, use directional drilling rather than trenching to minimize root damage. Assuming reasonably loose soil, it's fairly easy to dig a narrow channel under a concrete sidewalk, then run a metal pipe containing irrigation tubing under the walk, to connect a separate piece of land such as a parking strip to an irrigation system.

If your irrigation system is on an automatic timer, don't set it and forget it; adjust it with the seasons. Plants need more water during their peak growth, and overwatering at other times can promote disease and shorten their life spans.

Additional waterwise strategies discussed elsewhere in this book include mulching, vertical layering, earth-shaping, and building healthy soil, as well as choosing plants that are adapted to your climate and site.

Shrinking the Lawn

When you consider how to cut down your workload, evaluate any lawn area on your property where you only go to mow. Are you maintaining a perfect lawn that you never use? Even a relatively small section of turf on a hellstrip or slope could be causing a disproportionate share of your lawn chores. Conversely, are you neglecting a lawn that is struggling in harsh curbside conditions? You'll get a big payback from converting that high-need turf or that neglected plot to a landscape that stays appealing without so much help.

Converting lawn to garden takes a certain concentrated effort. The garden may need a few years of help and attention to get started. If well designed, it can grow to need less frequent care than the lawn's weekly mowings, perhaps just an intense work period once or twice a year, to keep it healthy and beautiful. It is more likely to

Freedom lawns make miniature meadows; this Cape Cod lawn sports early spring blooms of purple deadnettle (*Lamium purpureum*).

need informed, thoughtful intervention than lawn does. But whether it provides fresh strawberries for your plate or fragrant lilies for your vase, or the less tangible but no less valid joy of nurturing a living community, a garden's contribution to your quality of life can be priceless.

To remove an unwanted area of lawn, use a straight-edged shovel or hoe to cut lines in your lawn, then roll it up section by section and haul it away (to the compost pile). Rent a powered sod cutter, or buy or borrow a manual sod cutter, to make this process easier. The stripped area will be ready for planting right away, or you may want to replenish the topsoil before adding plants.

If it's really compacted and there are no trees in it, you could till it up, pull out the big chunks, and plant right away. Mulch heavily between plants to deter grass and weeds from regenerating or germinating. (Some will likely come up through the mulch anyway.)

Another method of killing the lawn is solarizing with black plastic, which blocks sunlight and water and can generate enough heat to kill weed seeds at the surface. Take up the plastic and plant directly into the dead lawn. This works well on a slope as the lawn's still-decomposing roots help stabilize soil against erosion while new plants are settling in.

Smothering with cardboard or newspaper topped with organic matter (leaves, pine needles, chipped wood)—though slower than the other methods—will create the best environment for your new plants because all the materials and your dying lawn attract soil life, which will decompose them into nutritious topsoil.

Alternatively, you might leave the lawn in place but change your maintenance practices and stop using fertilizers and other chemicals on it. These products applied to small strips of land can easily add their chemical burden to runoff, polluting lakes, streams, rivers, oceans, and groundwater.

The practice of "mowing what grows" creates a freedom lawn, which can be diverse and will evolve to be well adapted, with plants that persist despite mowing and without fertilizers, herbicides, or fungicides. Not only is it less costly, such a lawn also supports more pollinators and better soil health than a chemically maintained lawn. Children enjoy the diversity too: there may be bugs to watch, four-leaf clovers to find, onion grass to nibble, and flowers of violet, bugle, speedwell, and bluet for tiny bouquets. Plant with crocus, squill, muscari, windflowers, chinodoxa, and other little bulbs to put a spring in the step of pedestrians as they pass.

Trimming Waste

Some plants will need trimming and pruning, for aesthetics as well as for safety and convenience. Choose plants according to their expected mature size (or their expected size in five to ten years), and site them so they will not overreach their allotted space, to minimize the trimming they need.

When choosing a tree for a curbside location, consider the mature size of the tree and make sure the available root zone and soil quality of your site will meet its requirements. If you do not have the space for a tree, you might choose a larger shrub that can be limbed up into a short, multitrunked tree. Be aware that your city may regulate the species and placement of trees planted in parking strips and other easements.

Drought-tolerant evergreen silverleaf oak (*Quercus hypoleucoides*) grows slowly and produces very little litter while contributing four-season interest.

A yarrow rainbow works its magic, making a stump disappear.

As you are choosing plants, consider how you will handle the work and the cuttings they generate. To reduce waste and work, plan for trimmings to return to the garden. Easily degradable and fragile stems can be clipped or manually broken into small pieces and strewn around the plants where they will be hidden in the mulch and foliage. (This is a good job for helpful children.) Those that aren't chosen by birds for nest building will keep decomposers busy and will eventually return to your plants in a stream of slow-release nutrients.

Trimmings can also be added to your home compost. If they are cut in spring after standing all winter, they make ideal "brown" fibrous materials to balance the "green" fresh materials of kitchen scraps and newly weeded plants.

For larger quantities of material, design spaces into your garden where trimmings can slowly decompose. They might make a thick, effective, and free mulch under hedges and groups of shrubs, or around the edges of lawn islands to keep lawn grasses from running into planted areas.

Larger sticks and stalks can be used for brush piles, offering dens for animals and promoting growth of beneficial fungi. Site the piles far from house, deck, and bird feeder to lure small mammals away from those places. Add trimmed grasses and other seed stalks (sources of food) to keep the animals happy in that distant location.

Different types of trimmings suggest various crafts and projects: willow hoops or twig fences to edge planting beds or paths, hand-made trellises for climbing vines, fence posts, houses for birds and bats, insect hotels, fairy gardens, and other small construction projects.

If you must take down a tree, rather than paying to have it dug up (and your garden damaged by heavy machinery), consider leaving the stump as a garden structure—a pillar to display a potted plant or other garden art, a snag to feed woodpeckers, a custom-carved sculpture, a chair that doesn't get as cold as cement and won't be stolen. Stumps don't last forever, but they can be useful to you even as they are decomposing and feeding your soil.

In a prominent curbside garden, you may want to trim not only for plants' health but also for beauty—to promote rebloom or to remove plant tops that do not die gracefully. Timing will vary by species, and this is a good way to get to know each plant's seasonal rhythms.

Cliff green (*Paxistima canbyi*) makes a tidy low evergreen edge along a walkway and discourages unwanted plants from self-sowing under the hedge.

Where Paths Meet Plants

Paths of stone or gravel act as seedbeds for germination, and plants will eventually colonize the cracks of an unmortared path.

Here are various suggested techniques for making paved areas less prone to weeds:

- Remove plants and topsoil before installing paths and give them a well-compacted base.
- Combine different sizes of rock, from gravel to pea gravel to dust; this helps it to pack densely, filling more gaps and leaving fewer pockets where organic matter and water can collect and foster seedlings.
- Choose path materials that solidify as they are packed and wetted, such as sharp-edged class 5 limestone gravel.
- Sweep a mix of cement and sand into the cracks and gently water to make them less hospitable.
- Maintain unmortared pavement stretches by sweeping off leaves and other debris before they can contribute organic matter to the cracks.

Here are suggested strategies for dealing with unwanted plants in the cracks between paving stones or in gravel paths without using chemicals:

- Rake loose gravel frequently to impede seed germination and kill tiny seedlings.
- When plants appear, preferentially weed them to let desirable ones colonize.
- To kill seedlings, try burning with a fire wand (plumber's torch) or spraying with boiling water or garden-strength vinegar (acetic acid). Each of these methods requires careful attention to safety.
- Manual methods for killing seedlings include cutting to the ground (for those that won't resprout) and pulling by hand—or for wiry-stemmed tree seedlings, use a pair of pliers.
- Pull out larger plants manually.
- Paths of brick or paving stones can have all manner of mosses and small plants growing in them, and these can be periodically mown or trimmed, or simply walked on often to keep them low.

No-Blow Gardens

Preferring leaf blowers to rakes and brooms has led to noisier, more polluted landscapes. Though in some cases, a leaf blower may be the only effective tool (say, removing fallen leaves from a cactus garden or grooming a gravel walkway in a public park), using a rake or broom to maintain a modest-sized home landscape is healthier for plants and animals, and for people too.

Leaf blowers blow away not just leaves but also topsoil, exposing the ground to further erosion and colonization by windblown weed seeds. Blasts of hot, dry air (and the removal of protective organic matter from the top of the soil) destroy the top layer of soil microbial life, which is the most active in powering the soil food web.

Leaf blowers interfere with animals' ability to communicate with each other in order to find mates, to hunt, and to avoid predators. Removing leaf litter destroys the habitat of many beneficial and beautiful insects.

Use of leaf blowers threatens the hearing of their operators and anyone who happens to pass within 50 feet without wearing ear protection. Because they pollute the air, stirring up particulate matter, pollens, animal feces, landscape chemicals, lead, mold spores, and other respiratory irritants and allergens, the American Lung Association recommends avoiding them. Exhaust from gas-powered models releases carbon monoxide, nitrogen oxides, and hydrocarbons at higher levels than automobile exhaust.

Last but certainly not least, they shatter our peace. Exposure to noise can interrupt sleep, depress our immune systems, increase anxiety and hostility, lower productivity, aggravate heart disease, cause gastrointestinal distress, increase birth defects, and impair cognitive development in children.

Mary Hughes enjoys the quiet task of sweeping her Florida walk. "There are some real advantages, like spotting the early onset of weeds, seeing a struggling plant and giving it immediate help, and being able to hear compliments about the landscaping from passersby."

opposite Leadplant (*Amorpha canescens*) and other nitrogen fixers tolerate infertile sites and gently fertilize their companions.

In contrast, sweeping walkways (even gravel ones!) and raking leaves are healthy, pleasant outdoor activities that afford moderate exercise. This exercise is free, it can accomplish much of the work as quickly as leaf blowers would, and you can do it with the whole family. While you're at it, you can breathe the fresh air (rather than wearing a mask), converse and listen to birds and crickets (rather than wearing ear protection), and glory in the natural beauty of your garden.

Where you cannot accomplish the task with a manual tool, choose an electric rather than a gas-powered leaf blower. It will be quieter and emit no pollutants, though it will still generate dust, disturb soil, and produce enough heat to damage foliage and living organisms.

Building Healthy Soil

The key to thriving plants is a thriving soil food web. This underground network of organisms, mostly unnoticed by people, channels nutrients and water to plants while also aerating their root zone and protecting them from disease.

Soil organisms need food to do their jobs. Fallen leaves and other natural materials are their source of food. Cover the bare ground in your garden (or let it be covered) with plants and materials that feed the soil. A layer of fallen leaves will also buffer root zones against temperature extremes that can cause frost heaves and desiccation.

Building healthy soil means refraining from using synthetic fertilizers. These salt-based products strip soil of life, and that ultimately degrades its structure and its ability to hold water and nutrients. Instead, choose plants that won't need extra fertility and practices that will maintain healthy plant growth naturally.

Let nature help build your soil by incorporating nutrient-adding plants. Nitrogen fixers, including *Ceanothus* species, alder (*Alnus* species), false indigo (*Baptisia* species), bush clovers (*Lespedeza* species), lupines, clovers, and sweet peas, convert atmospheric nitrogen to a form they and their fellow plants can use. They drop their nitrogen-rich leaves year after year, and as their nitrogen-holding roots die back cyclically during fallow seasons, they improve overall soil health and increase the nutrients available to nearby plants. They grow easily in infertile soils and will flourish even as they improve a poor site.

Other soil builders are deep-rooted herbaceous perennials that reach into subsoil to find nutrients, then leave them at the surface when they die to the ground in fall. Different plants accumulate different nutrients. Comfrey (*Symphytum* species) has been used for generations as a grow-your-own soil improver (and a nutritious chicken feed). Slash the large, nutrient-rich leaves and pile on the ground where you want to improve soil fertility. Within a few days, they are crumbly and practically feel like rich, friable earth.

Working toward healthy soil means making room for mushrooms and other fungi in your garden. These decomposers perform the critical task of recycling nutrients to make them available for new plant growth. Key players in the soil food web, they form mutually beneficial relationships with your plants, funneling nutrients and disease-inhibiting substances to plant roots in exchange for carbohydrates and proteins that the roots exude.

To maintain its all-important structure, refrain from compacting your soil. Do not walk on it when it is wet. Sandy soils may recover from this but clay and loam will be compressed, destroying the network of pores that store air and water and harbor soil organisms.

Make paths to direct traffic through your garden and designate places where you always stand or step when maintaining it, be they working paths, stepping-stones, or just remembered spots. Once you have prepared and planted a garden, refrain from tilling or digging to keep the network of underground life intact, and in return it will continuously improve your soil.

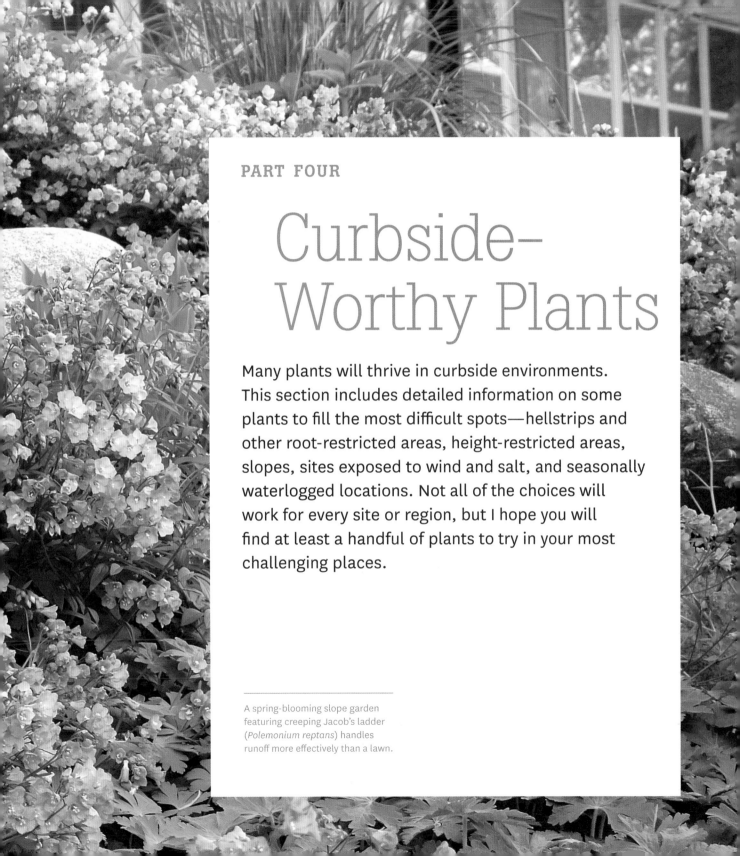

PART FOUR

Curbside–Worthy Plants

Many plants will thrive in curbside environments. This section includes detailed information on some plants to fill the most difficult spots—hellstrips and other root-restricted areas, height-restricted areas, slopes, sites exposed to wind and salt, and seasonally waterlogged locations. Not all of the choices will work for every site or region, but I hope you will find at least a handful of plants to try in your most challenging places.

A spring-blooming slope garden featuring creeping Jacob's ladder (*Polemonium reptans*) handles runoff more effectively than a lawn.

Plants with Showy Flowers

A curbside bed of showy dry-adapted flowers boasts sunset hyssop (*Agastache rupestris*), lemon-yellow yarrow (*Achillea*), and bright yellow black-eyed Susan (*Rudbeckia hirta*).

Acanthus spinosus
bear's breeches

Glossy leaves to 3 feet long form a mound supporting showy, wide towers of tubular white flowers with rose-green hoods that bloom all summer. Spiny, handle with care. Self-sows occasionally. Easily propagated from root pieces, hard to eradicate once planted. Bury in a pot to contain.

Preferences Tolerates drought and clay, but not poor-draining soil. Prefers part shade and average to moist soil. Wilts and dies down in hot southeastern summers. **Zones 5–9**

Achillea millefolium
yarrow

Fine-leaved, aromatic foliage 2 feet high spreads by rhizomes to form dense patches. Self-sows abundantly. Species is white flowered; cultivars include reds, pinks, and yellows. Foliage tolerates mowing and foot traffic. Can be grown in an occasionally mowed flowering field or as a regularly cut herbal lawn.

Preferences Poor, dry soil and full sun. Needs good drainage.
Zones 3–9

Alcea rosea
hollyhock

Low mounds of large, scalloped leaves form flower stalks 3 to 6 feet tall in their second year. Showy single flowers of white, pink, or red bloom all summer, attracting hummingbirds and pollinators. Tolerates juglone and drought. Biennial, but reseeding colonies persist. Easy from seed.

Preferences Full sun. Needs winter drainage.
Zones 2–10

Allium azureum
blue of the heavens

Heirloom bulb produces hollow, blade-shaped leaves 12 to 24 inches tall that die back before the flowers. Stiff 2-foot stems support round, vivid blue flower heads in very late spring. Self-sows readily.

Preferences Tolerates summer drought. Requires spring moisture.
Zones 3–8

Amorpha canescens
leadplant

Deep-rooted, nitrogen-fixing plant native to central North America is technically a shrub, but very little structure remains in winter. Several thin, woody stems with pinnate, felty silver foliage form a loose group to 3 feet tall and wide. Spikes of purple flowers with orange anthers emerge in mid- to late summer. Takes a few years to develop. Good bee plant.

Preferences Dry, alkaline soil and light to part shade. Needs good drainage. **Zones 2–9**

Amsonia hubrichtii
bluestar

Long, narrow, pointed leaves radiate from upright stems to form a dense, fine-textured tower of foliage that turns golden orange in autumn. Pale blue late spring flowers emerge above the foliage in loose conical clusters. Attracts butterflies. Native to south-central United States. Height and spread 2 to 3 feet.

Preferences Moderate moisture. Sun to part shade. **Zones 5–8**

Anemone cylindrica
thimbleweed

Low mound of deeply lobed foliage a foot across sends up flower stalks in spring. Small white cones of flowers turn to fluffy seed heads, nesting material for small birds. Native to northern, central, and eastern North America.

Preferences Full to part sun. Dry to moist sandy soil. Tolerates drought. **Zones 2–8**

Baptisia 'Purple Smoke'

Asclepias tuberosa
butterfly weed

All summer, flat flower clusters of dazzling orange adorn the dark green lance-shaped leaves of this 2-foot perennial butterfly magnet, native to eastern and southern North America. Attracts color-coordinated aphids to feed the ladybugs. After blooming, it produces long narrow pods that split to release dark seeds packed in white fluff, which is used by some birds for nest building. Valuable pollinator plant and larval host for monarch, gray hairstreak, and queen butterflies.

Preferences Full sun, dry to moderate moisture. Prefers good drainage. Very drought tolerant. Tolerates alkaline and clay soils. **Zones 3–9**

Baptisia australis
blue false indigo

Deep-rooted clump of stems with trifoliate, blue-green leaves grows to 3 to 4 feet tall and wide. Long, loose cones of pealike blue flowers rise well above the foliage in early summer and attract pollinators. Develops showy, dusty blue-black seedpods that rattle when dried. Nitrogen fixer, deep rooted, native to eastern and south-central United States. Takes several years to develop. 'Purple Smoke' is a hybrid of *Baptisia australis* and the native American *B. alba*, combining the blue-purple flowers of *B. australis* with the smaller stature and contrasting stems of *B. alba*.

Preferences Well-drained soil and full sun. Tolerates drought, clay, and part shade. Resents relocation. **Zones 3–10**

Callirhoe involucrata
winecups

Deeply lobed leaves on trailing stems grow densely to 1 foot high and several feet wide. Produces abundant, cup-shaped flowers of deep magenta with white centers from spring through midsummer. Translucent petals glow in sunlight. Good companion for taller plants with long legs. Easy to grow, may self-sow. Native to central United States. Nectar plant for pollinators, larval host for gray hairstreak.

Preferences Sun to part shade. Needs good drainage. Tolerates a wide range of soils including clay. Resents transplanting once established. **Zones 4–8**

Coreopsis verticillata
threadleaf coreopsis

Long-blooming mound of needled foliage 3 feet tall and broad is covered with bright yellow daisy-shaped flowers from summer into fall. Seeds attract birds, nectar attracts butterflies and other pollinators. Native to eastern United States. Spreads by rhizomes and self-sowing.

Preferences Full sun. Tolerates acidic conditions, dry and infertile soil, heat, humidity, and drought. Prefers fast-draining soil. **Zones 3–9**

Epilobium canum
California fuchsia, zauschneria

Profuse orange-red tubular flowers late summer into fall furnish late-season nectar, fueling hummingbird migration. Native to western United States. Shrubby, to 2 feet high and 3 to 4 feet wide.

Preferences Drought tolerant. **Zones 8–10**

Kniphofia 'Christmas Cheer'

Geranium macrorrhizum
big-root geranium

Semi-evergreen 2-foot mound of deeply lobed leaves glows red-orange-scarlet in fall. Blooms pink to purple late spring through midsummer. Rhizomatous, self-sows freely. Attracts pollinators. Effective erosion control, good companion under trees. Similar but lower, bloody cranesbill (*Geranium sanguineum*) has larger magenta flowers.

Preferences Sun to part shade. Tolerates dry soil and roadside pollution.
Zones 3–8

Kniphofia cultivars
red hot poker

One-foot mound of broad straplike leaves grows to 2 feet wide. In midsummer, tight cones of tubular flowers rise on sturdy stalks a foot above the foliage. Cultivars bloom in a range of warm colors from yellow to orange to red, some varieties two-toned. May need winter protection in cooler zones.

Preferences Full sun. Dry to moderate moisture. Drought tolerant. Does not tolerate wet soil.
Zones 5–9, depending on variety

Liatris punctata
dotted blazing star

Deep-rooted and long-lived, this is the most drought-tolerant liatris. From late summer to mid-autumn, purple-pink 16- to 30-inch flower spikes attract bees and butterflies. Nectar fuels migrating monarchs. Sturdy clusters of seed stalks stand through winter to feed small birds. Native to central North America.

Preferences Full sun. Tolerates alkaline soils, clay, and heat. Needs good drainage.
Zones 3–9

Linum perenne
perennial blue flax

A 12- to 16-inch cloud of pale green needle-leaved foliage supports yellow-centered sky-blue flowers. Self-sows readily. Mingles well with plants of similar or shorter stature, even sun lovers. North American native *L. lewisii* is similar in culture and appearance.

Preferences Full sun to part shade, good drainage. Very tolerant of drought, heat, and humidity. May not overwinter in clay soils. **Zones 5–8**

Penstemon pinifolius
pineleaf penstemon

Year-round stalks of coniferous-looking foliage are green to burgundy in winter. Produces tubular orange-red flowers through summer and fall. Attracts birds, bees, butterflies, and hummingbirds. Native to southwestern United States.

Preferences Full sun to light shade, regular but sparse moisture. Loves heat. Alkaline to acidic soil. **Zones 4–9**

Polemonium reptans
creeping Jacob's ladder, Greek valerian

Loose mound grows to 12 to 16 inches tall and wide with paired oval leaves along arched stalks. Despite the name, does not creep. Native to eastern North America. Blooms in midspring with sky-blue elongated flowers that native bees favor. Self-sows in optimal conditions. Will go dormant in drought.

Preferences Sun (in cooler climates) to mostly shade. Moist to average, rich, well-drained soil. **Zones 3–8**

Ruellia humilis
wild petunia

Oblong, hairy gray-green leaves form dense clusters of erect stems 12 to 16 inches high. Native to eastern United States. Produces trumpet-shaped, light purple-pink flowers summer through fall. Self-sows where happy. Attracts long-tongued bees and hummingbirds.

Preferences Dry to average moisture, well-drained soil, full sun to part shade. **Zones 4–9**

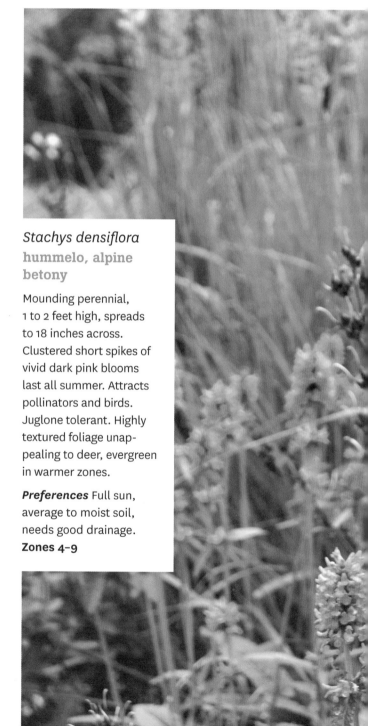

Salvia pachyphylla
Mojave sage

Silver-green, fuzzy, very aromatic oval leaves that deer detest line thick stems growing in a loose cluster to 36 inches tall and wide. From midsummer to fall, stalks are topped with pink-purple spiky flowers that attract hummingbirds and bees. Native to southwestern United States. Evergreen. Self-sows in ideal conditions.

Preferences Full sun to light shade. Dry soil with occasional water.
Zones 6–9

Scutellaria suffrutescens
cherry skullcap

Forms a carpet 6 to 12 inches high, to 2 feet across, making a good ground cover under taller plants. Lipped, tubular red-pink flowers bloom early summer through fall. Attracts bees and hummingbirds.

Preferences Full sun to part shade. Tolerates drought, heat, and competition from tree roots. Dry to average soil with occasional water.
Zones 7–10

Stachys densiflora
hummelo, alpine betony

Mounding perennial, 1 to 2 feet high, spreads to 18 inches across. Clustered short spikes of vivid dark pink blooms last all summer. Attracts pollinators and birds. Juglone tolerant. Highly textured foliage unappealing to deer, evergreen in warmer zones.

Preferences Full sun, average to moist soil, needs good drainage.
Zones 4–9

Veronica spicata 'Red Fox'

Symphyotrichum oblongifolium
aromatic aster

Stiff, multibranched stems grow thickly 14 to 18 inches tall. Small, narrow leaves have a light minty aroma when crushed. Lavender-blue flowers with gold centers bloom profusely in fall, fueling butterfly migrations and pollinators. Birds eat seeds. Native to central and eastern United States. Slowly spreads by stolons. Prune to keep low and thick, or it may sprawl. Works well on slopes.

Preferences Dry to moist soil, sun to part shade, good drainage. Tolerates drought, infertility, and alkaline soil. **Zones 3–8**

Veronica spicata
spiked speedwell

Spikes of bloom 16 to 20 inches tall rise from a lower mound of fresh green lance-shaped leaves. Blooms range from purple to blue to pink. Native to northeastern North America. 'Red Fox' (synonym 'Rotfuchs') is a compact grower with low basal rosette and 15-inch flower spikes of deep rose.

Preferences Well-drained soil, full sun to part shade. **Zones 3–8**

plants with showy flowers · 231

Plants with Showy Foliage

A trio of contrasts: strappy sweet flag (*Acorus gramineus*), textured low juniper, and sculptural thornless prickly pear (*Opuntia ellisiana*) border the walk at Daniel Stowe Botanical Garden.

Acorus gramineus
sweet flag

Fresh yellow-green, aromatic blades form arching mounds 1 foot tall and wide. Evergreen in warmer zones. Slowly and indefinitely spreads by rhizomes. Good erosion control and understory plant for rain gardens, woodland gardens, shorelines, and stream banks. Golden-leaved 'Minimus Aureus' grows only 3 inches tall, slowly spreads to 2 feet wide in five years, takes light foot traffic.

Preferences Part sun to dense shade. Likes consistently moist soil and tolerates waterlogged soil; will scorch in dry soil. Protect from afternoon sun in warmer zones. **Zones 5–9**

Anemone canadensis

Canada anemone

Herbaceous perennial with deeply lobed leaves spreads rhizomatously to form dense colonies a foot high, with white open-faced flowers interspersed in early summer. Native to northern United States and Canada.

Preferences Part to full shade, average to moist soil. **Zones 2–9**

Antennaria parvifolia

dwarf pussytoes

Mat-forming walkable ground cover native to western and central North America has silvery white, furry foliage. In late summer, produces short stalks topped with flat white flower heads. Larval host for painted lady butterfly.

Preferences Extremely drought and heat tolerant. Likes dry, well-drained soil in full sun to part shade. **Zones 4–9**

Artemisia 'Powis Castle'

wormwood

Silver-toned, feathery, extremely aromatic foliage forms a cloud 2 feet high. Sprawls in humidity or shade. Evergreen. Can spread by rhizomes to 3 to 6 feet across. Related curlicue sage (*Artemisia versicolor* 'Sea Foam') is smaller, growing to 12 inches high and 3 feet across, with blue foliage.

Preferences Full sun to light shade, infertile soil with dry to medium moisture. Needs excellent drainage. Drought tolerant. **Zones 6–9**

Astelia nervosa

mountain astelia

Mound of straplike green-gray leaves grows 1 to 2 feet high and spreads to several feet across. Evergreen.

Preferences Moist, rich soil and protection from direct sun and strong wind. Tolerates salt and clay soil. **Zones 9–11**

Bouteloua gracilis 'Blonde Ambition'

Carex morrowii 'Silver Sceptre'

Bouteloua gracilis
blue grama

Fine-bladed warm-season grass with a gray-blue cast stays under 12 inches high. Native to North America, it is a bunchgrass in southern areas, but forms sod in cooler regions. In summer, eyelash-shaped horizontal seed heads wave at the tips of wiry stems; birds eat the seeds. Foliage turns bright tan in fall, remains through winter, giving a long season of interest. Grows easily from seed. Can be seeded as a lawn and mowed, and will withstand regular foot traffic. Big blue grama ('Blonde Ambition'), larger and showy, grows 24 to 36 inches tall, with wiry blue-green stems that support bright yellow-tan eyelash-shaped seed heads.

Preferences Full sun. Drought resistant. Tolerates low fertility but not acidic soil. **Zones 4–9**

Carex morrowii
Japanese sedge

One-foot-tall mound of straplike, narrow, semi-evergreen foliage spreads to 2 feet. Brown seed heads are held aloft from spring through midsummer. Great for rain garden understory and erosion control in shady wooded areas. Will spread to naturalize. 'Variegata' has a white linear band along the center of each leaf, lighting up a shady area. 'Silver Sceptre' has wider blades that are green with white edges.

Preferences Part to dense shade, moist to wet soil. Tolerates waterlogged soil. **Zones 5–9**

Carex testacea 'Prairie Fire'

Carex testacea
New Zealand sedge

Olive-green, fine-bladed, clump-forming cool-season grass grows 12 to 16 inches tall and wide. Leaves turn orange to warm brown in cooler weather. 'Prairie Fire' has a bronze to orange fall color lasting through winter.

Preferences Filtered sun to shade. Requires good drainage and consistent moisture. **Zones 5–9**

Caulophyllum thalictroides
blue cohosh

Native to eastern North America, this herbaceous perennial has horizontal panels of lobed blue-green leaves spreading to 1 foot wide on upright stems 12 to 30 inches high. Short sprays of tiny yellow-green flowers arch above in spring. Clusters of deep blue berries, which are poisonous, appear in summer and remain after leaf fall. Spreads very slowly by rhizomes.

Preferences Dappled to dense shade. Rich, consistently moist soil. **Zones 3–8**

Chasmanthium latifolium
river oats

Clump-forming cool-season perennial grass native to eastern, central, and southern United States emerges early. Blue-green 6-inch straplike leaves jut out along its wiry stalks. Grows to 2 to 4 feet tall. Prominent dangling seed heads start pale green and turn to ivory, then tan, and finally gray in late winter. Seeds provide food for birds; the plant is a larval host to several butterflies. Easy to grow from seed. Naturalizes well on stream banks and in moist, shady areas.

Preferences Part to full shade. Tolerates waterlogged soil. Thrives in dry shade throughout much of the continent, including coastal areas. **Zones 4–9**

Dichondra argentea
silver ponyfoot

Prostate grower with round silver-blue leaves on sprawling stems stays under 6 inches high and spreads to 3 feet across. Native to south-central United States. Good under and among taller plants. Metallic in full sun.

Preferences Dry soil, good drainage, full sun to part shade. **Zones 9–11**

Geum fragarioides
barren strawberry

Evergreen ground cover less than 6 inches high spreads by rhizomes. Native to eastern United States, it blooms during spring, with showy single yellow flowers held slightly aloft dotted over its thick green mat of foliage. Bears small, inedible fruits. Good living mulch under taller plants in a hellstrip; controls erosion on slopes.

Preferences Sun to shade. Average moisture, well-drained soil. Tolerates drought but not hot, humid summers. **Zones 4–7**

Hakonechloa macra 'Aureola'

Hakonechloa macra
Japanese forest grass

Low, dense, mounding, wide-bladed grass with green-yellow variegation grows 14 to 24 inches tall and to 3 feet across. Sprays of light purple flowers turning to dark tan seeds arch out from centers of leaf blades in mid to late summer. Spreads slowly. 'Aureola' has a golder tint than the species, with yellow-green flowers, and stays 14 to 16 inches tall.

Preferences Needs consistent moisture and light to moderate shade. Protect from direct sun in hotter climates. Tolerates juglone, pollution.
Zones 5–9

Helictotrichon sempervirens
blue oat grass

Showy medium-sized cool-season grass. Striking thick mound of fine pale blue blades with fountaining form grows 2 to 3 feet tall and broad. Densely clustered cones of seeds are pale tan and held several inches above the foliage. Looks like a larger version of blue fescue (*Festuca glauca*).

Preferences Dry to medium soil in full sun to some shade. Tolerates juglone, drought, pollution. **Zones 4–8**

Leptinella squalida
'Platt's Black'

Heuchera micrantha
coral bells

Herbaceous perennial native to western North America has ruffled, slightly lobed leaves that form a thick mound 14 to 18 inches high and wide. Dark, wiry stems arch over the foliage, holding conelike sprays of tiny flowers, in late spring to early summer. Reproduces by forming detachable plantlets at the base and, rarely, self-sowing. Many cultivars are available, with varying leaf sizes and colors from green to purple to dark apricot, flowers from white to bright pink to red. 'Palace Purple' leaves are colored dull to rich purple with red undersides; flower sprays are shell pink. Several other species native to different parts of North America are similar.

Preferences Part shade, fluffy organic soil, regular moisture. Tolerates root competition from trees. **Zones 4–9**

Heuchera 'Cherry Cola'

Leptinella squalida
brass buttons

Flat, feathery leaved, bright green mat former spreads indefinitely by rhizomes. Gold flowers in summer are followed by tiny fruit. Somewhat walkable. Useful between paving stones or as a lawn alternative. Evergreen in warmer regions. 'Platt's Black' leaves are dark brown mixed with green.

Preferences Full sun to part shade. Moderately moist, well-drained soils. **Zones 4–10**

Marrubium rotundifolium
roundleaf horehound

Dense mat of fuzzy white stems and round green leaves with white furred undersides grows to a foot high and 3 feet across. Stalks with white, insignificant flowers rise several inches above in spring and give a looser look; can be sheared to produce a more uniform carpet of foliage. Evergreen.

Preferences Full sun. Tolerates drought and many soil types. Needs good drainage. Rots in high humidity. **Zones 4–9**

Muhlenbergia reverchonii 'Undaunted'

Oenothera fremontii 'Shimmer'

Muhlenbergia reverchonii
seep muhly

Warm-season grass with extremely narrow-bladed foliage forms clumps to 2 feet wide and tall. Clouds of tiny pink flowers turning to silver float above in late summer through fall. Tawny winter color. Self-sows occasionally. Native to south-central United States, it is the most cold hardy *Muhlenbergia* species. 'Undaunted' was introduced by the Ogdens.

Preferences Tolerates drought, heat, infertile soils, and alkalinity. Needs good drainage. Full sun to light shade. **Zones 5–10**

Oenothera fremontii
narrow-leaf evening primrose

Silvery, narrow, lance-shaped leaves of this herbaceous perennial native to the western United States radiate from stems, forming a loose mound 6 inches tall and a foot across. Produces large yellow, papery thin four-petaled flowers throughout summer. Good low plant for the front of the border. Native to western United States. 'Shimmer', introduced by the Ogdens, has striking silvery blue foliage that is extremely fine-textured.

Preferences Full sun, dry to moderate moisture. **Zones 4–8**

Onoclea sensibilis
sensitive fern

Deeply lobed bright green fronds 3 to 4 feet long grow in a mound to 3 feet across. Deciduous. Woody brown stalks to a foot tall persist through winter. Native to eastern and central North America. Will naturalize by spores and creeping rhizomes where happy. Good in rain gardens, tree islands, and for stabilizing stream banks and shorelines.

Preferences Part to dense shade. Rich, well-drained soil with regular moisture. Tolerates clay soil. **Zones 4–8**

Ophiopogon japonicus 'Nana'

Ophiopogon planiscapus
mondo grass

Grasslike bladed foliage forms a 6-to-8-inch-high turf, spreading slowly and indefinitely. Foliage remains through winter in warmer zones. Can be mowed and walked on, used as a lawn substitute. 'Nigrescens' (black mondo) has black foliage with inconspicuous pink flowers hidden in the leaves in late summer, followed by small black berries. *Ophiopogon japonicus* 'Nana' grows just 3 inches high, with dark green foliage, and makes a low-care, no-mow lawn that withstands moderate, regular foot traffic.

Preferences Full sun to part shade. Prefers consistent moisture and good drainage. Drought tolerant. **Zones 6–9**

Pachysandra procumbens
Allegheny spurge

Herbaceous ground cover, native to southeastern United States, grows 8 to 12 inches tall and spreads slowly and indefinitely by long, rooting stems 2 to 3 feet outward from each central root mass. Blue-green, horizontally overlapping leaves may be mottled in late summer with flecks of silver and purple. Foliage dies back in cooler zones, remains through winter in warmer zones. New leaves emerge above root masses. Produces short white-pink spikes of fragrant flowers in early to mid-spring. Great ground cover under shrubs and trees, on shady slopes, as nonwalkable lawn alternative.

Preferences Dappled to dense shade, moderate water. Prefers rich, acidic, well-drained soil. **Zones 4–10**

Panicum virgatum
switch grass

This clump-forming warm-season grass is native throughout North America. Thin, wiry stalks 3 to 6 feet high open to loose, airy panicles of pink-tinted seed heads in midsummer. Foliage turns glowing gold with orange overtones in fall, bright tan through winter. Will naturalize by self-sowing and spreading rhizomatously. Good for rain gardens and shoreline erosion control. Birds eat seeds.

Preferences Full sun to some shade, average to wet soil. Tolerates drought, pollution, and juglone. Prefers clay soil. Grows more erect in infertile soil. **Zones 5–9**

Panicum virgatum 'Shenandoah'

· 243

Phormium colensoi (synonym *P. cookianum*)
New Zealand mountain flax

Smaller of two New Zealand flax species (the other is *Phormium tenax*). Broad, straplike evergreen leaves from green to bronze to pink-brown form an arching mound 15 to 18 inches high. Produces occasional inconspicuous yellow-green flowers on arching stalks. Named cultivars have bands of various colors lengthwise along the leaves. Leaves dry to soft gold and can be used to weave baskets and mats. Cut leaves and discard the midribs, then use as ties for staked and trellis-growing plants. Related New Zealand coastal flax (*P. tenax*) is similar but larger and a more upright grower, with occasional red or orange flowers held above foliage on sturdy 3-foot stalks.

Preferences Light shade. Moderately dry soil. Tolerates salt and clay.
Zones 8–11

Phormium 'Maori Sunrise'

Salvia argentea
silver sage

Biennial has a basal rosette to 1 foot high and 3 feet across of thick, woolly white leaves that are 8 to 12 inches long. Stalks of tubular white flowers rise above leaves in summer of second year. Plant will die after flowering but can persist if flower stalks are clipped as they appear. May self-sow. Touchable, great for children's gardens.

Preferences Full sun and moderate moisture. Tolerates drought. Needs good drainage. Foliage declines in humid, hot weather. **Zones 5–8**

Saxifraga stolonifera
strawberry begonia

Broadleaf evergreen mounding perennial reaches 10 to 14 inches high and wide. Striking white and green variegated heart-shaped leaves echo the bright white flowers dangling from wiry stalks a foot above them, making this plant glow in a shady area. Undersides of leaves are pinkish red. Prefers protection from winter cold. Produces plantlets via aboveground runners, in the manner of strawberries, and will naturalize fairly rapidly.

Preferences Part to full shade, medium moisture, good winter drainage. **Zones 6–9**

Schizachyrium scoparium 'The Blues'

Schizachyrium scoparium
little bluestem

Clump-forming warm-season grass native to eastern North America grows 2 to 4 feet tall and 1 to 2 feet wide. Silvery green stems turn purple-red in late summer and are tipped with fluffy white seed heads. Deep-rooted, effective at erosion control. Works at the sunny, drier edge of a rain garden. Birds eat seeds.

Preferences Full sun to very light shade, dry to moderate moisture. Tolerates drought, pollution, and juglone. **Zones 3–9**

Sedum rupestre
stonecrop, creeping sedum

Short, tightly packed towers of gray-green, succulent foliage 3 to 6 inches high spread to 1 to 2 feet across. Bright yellow star-shaped flower clusters rise a few inches above the foliage all summer. Evergreen foliage may redden in cold winters. Will naturalize over time. 'Angelina' has golden yellow foliage all summer, striking burnt-orange in autumn in colder regions.

Preferences Full sun to light shade. Needs good drainage. Tolerates drought, pollution, heat, and infertility. **Zones 5–8**

Sedum rupestre 'Angelina'

Symphytum ×uplandicum 'Axminster Gold'

Symphytum ×uplandicum
Russian comfrey

Large, wide, blade-shaped leaves with a coarse, puckery surface form a dense, upright mound to 3 to 4 feet high and 3 feet wide. Early summer stalks of dangling blue-purple bell-shaped flowers attract bees, butterflies, and hummingbirds. Useful hedge to contain spreading plants including lawn. Very deep taproot, hard to eradicate. Sprouts from root pieces. Different selections spread assertively by rhizomes. 'Axminster Gold' has wide creamy striping along leaf edges.

Preferences Full sun, some afternoon shade in hotter zones. Drought tolerant once established. Tolerates pollution and poor or contaminated soils.
Zones 4–8

Tanacetum densum
partridge feather

Dense mat 6 to 12 inches tall spreads slowly to 2 feet across. Overlapping white fuzzy leaves look like feathers. Evergreen. Yellow button-like flowers emerge above foliage in early to mid-summer. Foliage may irritate some people's skin. Attracts butterflies.

Preferences Full sun; dry, well-drained soil. Tolerates heat, drought. Humidity rots the foliage.
Zones 4–9

Plants with Culinary or Medicinal Uses

A waterfall of sweet potato vine (*Ipomoea batatas*, golden 'Marguerite' and purple 'Blackie'), the leaves and tuberous roots of which are edible, flows over a curbside retaining wall.

Many plants and their parts—leaves, fibers, berries and nuts, roots, stems—are useful to people. Enjoy edible and medicinal plants mingled among the other plants in your garden, or segregate them for convenient care and harvesting. Here are some to try.

Note that not all these plants are edible; some are actually poisonous, and those that are edible may also have poisonous parts. Moreover, people have unique physiological responses to different plants; foods and medicinals that some find pleasant and effective may be unpalatable, intolerable, or harmful to others. When trying an unfamiliar food, do your research to make sure you are harvesting and preparing it correctly, and always start with a small portion to test your individual response. The best guide is often someone who has successfully used the plant as food or medicine.

Agastache rupestris
sunset hyssop

This herbaceous perennial is native to the southwestern United States. Clumps of aromatic, threadlike foliage grow to 2 to 3 feet tall. Small tubular flowers in sunset hues attract hummingbirds, butterflies, and bees midsummer to fall. Leaves make a sweet, mint-flavored tea.

Preferences Moderately dry soil, part to full sun. Tolerates drought and infertile soils. **Zones 4–10**

Aloe vera
aloe vera

Blue-gray succulent leaves make an erect rosette 24 to 30 inches tall. Evergreen foliage is purple tinted in winter. Reproduces by forming "pups" next to the parents that can be pulled off and used as starts. Not edible, but grow your own soothing balm; break apart a stem and smear the clear gel on sunburns, burns, and stings. Plant in pots and bring outdoors for the summer. Attracts hummingbirds. Good firescaping plant. 'Blue Elf' takes low light, grows 8 to 12 inches tall, and blooms red in winter with intermittent repeats year-round.

Preferences Filtered light or afternoon shade in hot desert regions. Moderately fertile, fast-draining soil. Drought tolerant. Dies in frost. **Zones 9–11**

Asimina triloba 'Wilson'

Amelanchier ×grandiflora 'Autumn Brilliance'

Amelanchier laevis
Allegheny serviceberry

Small multitrunked tree or large shrub native to eastern and central North America grows 15 to 25 feet tall with smooth pale gray bark. Offers early spring flowers for pollinators, red-tinted new leaves, pitless purple-red edible summer berries that look like blueberries and taste like cherry-almond. Foliage turns orange-red in fall. Birds and small mammals eat the berries as soon as they ripen. Useful rain garden plant. Similar to *Amelanchier arborea. Amelanchier ×grandiflora* 'Autumn Brilliance' is a cross between the two species.

Preferences Moderate moisture. Sun to part shade. Tolerates pollution and periodic flooding. **Zones 3–9**

Asimina triloba
pawpaw

Short tree native to eastern and central United States reaches 15 to 25 feet tall with large, pendant leaves 6 to 12 inches long. Species suckers to produce multiple trunks, forming groves. Autumn foliage is pale to golden yellow. Purple-brown, bowl-shaped flowers emerge before the leaves. Trees are either male or female (that is, they are dioecious); females produce oblong yellow-to-orange edible fruits with a strong fragrance. Fruits may fall before ripe; collect and ripen before eating. Custardy inner flesh can be eaten raw (sans seeds) or used in smoothies, pies, puddings. Good under mature trees, on north and east sides of buildings, and in low wet places and shady rain gardens. Larval host for zebra swallowtail butterfly and pawpaw sphinx moth.

Preferences Part to dense shade. Moderate to moist soils, slightly acidic. Tolerates clay and periodic flooding. Protect from winds and afternoon sun. **Zones 5–9**

Lacinato kale

Brassica oleracea
kale

Highly nutritious single-stalked broccoli relative grows to 3 feet tall and half as wide. Flowers and dies in the second year; planted as an annual for culinary use. Average 30 days to harvestable baby leaves, 65 days to mature. Early new leaves are good as salad greens. Leaves add flavor to soups and stews; sauté with oil or butter and add to grain or pasta dishes. After frost, flavor is sweeter. Harvest leaves individually to keep a show going in your garden. Tuscan (lacinato) kale is an Italian heirloom variety with dark blue-green, puckery leaves; 'Redbor' has curly dark purple leaves and a lighter purple stalk.

Preferences Best in part shade. Extremely frost tolerant and can continue producing new growth through winters in zones 7–10. **Zones 1–10**

Calendula officinalis
pot marigold

One- to 2-foot mound of aromatic foliage produces single-stalked orange-yellow flowers that bloom from summer until frost. Edible, somewhat bitter flowers and leaves. Petals used in topical applications for minor wounds, burns, and general skin health. Commonly grown as an annual in cooler zones. May self-sow, easy from seed. Attracts butterflies.

Preferences Sunny, rich, well-drained soil. Tolerates juglone. Frost tender. **Zones 8–11**

Calluna vulgaris
heather

Evergreen shrub forms a thick mat of foliage 1 to 2 feet high and wide that is gray to green in spring/summer, bronze to purple through fall/winter. Showy pink to white blooms from summer into fall. Superb bee plant. Flower tops make pleasant, soothing tea or aromatic ale and can be added to baths to ease aches. Naturalized in northeastern and northwestern North America; classified as

Cercis occidentalis

Ficus carica 'Sticky Fingers'

Cercis canadensis
eastern redbud

invasive in some coastal states. For a native substitute, try salal (*Gaultheria shallon*), with sweet edible berries and edible young leaves.

Preferences Full sun to part shade. Lean, acidic soil with regular moisture and good drainage. Protect from hot afternoon sun. Dislikes humidity, clay, root disturbance, and wind. **Zones 3–10, varies widely by cultivar**

Fast-growing, small deciduous tree to 15 to 25 feet tall and broad with heart-shaped leaves. Purple-pink fragrant flowers stud bare branches in early spring; flowers and buds are edible, slightly sour, and can be eaten raw in salads, stir fried, or used to flavor baked goods. Flat purple-gray pods may persist through winter. Nitrogen fixer, native to eastern North America. Valuable to birds, butterflies, and bumble bees. For sunny, dry, well-drained sites

in warmer regions, consider similar *Cercis canadensis* var. *texensis* (Texas redbud) or *C. occidentalis* (western redbud).

Preferences Light shade to full sun (may need shade in hottest part of summer). Acid to alkaline soil, moist with good drainage. Tolerates drought once established. Tolerates clay and juglone. **Zones 5–9 eastern redbud, 6–9 Texas redbud, 7–10 western redbud**

Ficus carica
fig

Large, broad-crowned, deciduous shrub reaches 15 feet tall and 20 feet wide. Dark green, leathery, deeply lobed leaves vaguely resemble human hands. Dies to ground in winter in colder zones. Sticky brown fruits are edible raw and have many culinary uses including confections and sauces. Birds also enjoy them.

Preferences Full to part sun. Average to moist soil. Tolerates heat, humidity, drought. **Zones 6–9**

Fragaria chiloensis
beach strawberry

Evergreen perennial native to western North America, 6 to 12 inches high with clusters of trifoliate dark green leaves, spreads indefinitely and densely by rooting aboveground runners to form new plantlets. Produces white flowers with yellow centers in spring and early summer, followed by edible red berries. Holds sandy soil well against erosion. Attracts birds. Tolerates moderate, regular foot traffic.

Preferences Light to full shade. Sandy, well-drained soils with regular moisture. Protect from hot afternoon sun.
Zones 4–9

Ipomoea batatas 'Marguerite'

Ipomoea batatas
sweet potato

Vining tender perennial is grown as an annual in colder zones. Deeply lobed leaves are green in species, with gold, variegated, and purple cultivars available. Spreads by trailing stems that root where they touch soil, or can be trained up a trellis. Species occasionally produces pink-purple trumpet-shaped flowers. Extensive roots produce edible tubers; leaves are also edible, although palatability of all parts varies widely depending on cultivar. 'Marguerite' is the most productive gold-leaved cultivar, and 'Blackie' is a popular purple-leaved one.

Preferences Full sun, consistently moist soil. Frost intolerant.
Zones 9–11

Lablab purpureus
lablab

With heart-shaped leaves and showy flowers, lablab is an annual vine reaching 10 feet in colder zones, a 30-foot woody perennial in warmer zones. Bright purple beans are edible when young but contain toxins when dried. Naturalizes. Nitrogen fixer.

Preferences Needs sun, good drainage. Tolerates poor soil and drought. **Zones 10–11**

Mahonia repens
creeping Oregon grape

Low, spreading broadleaf evergreen shrub stays less than a foot high and is native to northwestern North America. Leathery green, spiny, hollylike leaves are purple-tinted in winter. Showy clusters of yellow spring flowers are followed by equally showy clusters of small dusty blue fruits, which are sour but edible in jellies. Easy-care understory for tree islands.

Preferences: Full sun to nearly full shade, medium moisture, good drainage. Acidic soil. **Zones 5–8**

Monarda fistulosa
wild bergamot

North American native with erect, sturdy stalks bearing pointed felty green leaves forms a dense cluster 2 to 3 feet tall and wide. Flat heads of arched tubular lavender-colored flowers bloom midsummer into fall. Aromatic leaves make a pleasant minty-flavored tea. Edible leaves and flowers can be added to salads. May self-sow. Attracts hummingbirds, butterflies, and hummingbird moths.

Related bee balm (*Monarda didyma*), used as a tea by colonists during the Boston Tea Party rebellion, has crimson flowers and similar cultivation and uses but requires consistently moist soil and good air circulation to perform well.

Preferences: Sun to part shade. Any soil type and moisture level. Tolerates clay, juglone, and drought. **Zones 3–9**

Pennisetum glaucum 'Purple Majesty'

Opuntia ellisiana
spineless prickly pear

Evergreen cactus native to Texas features a sculptural agglomeration of rounded succulent blue-green pads. No large quills, but avoid touching clusters of tiny sliverlike thorns dotting the pads. Large, frilly blooms with translucent petals in red, pink, orange, or yellow open in early summer; some are fragrant. Valuable to native bees. Produces tasty, edible, bright red fruits called tunas. Good focal point for meadows and shorter planted borders.

Preferences Very drought tolerant. Sun to part shade, dry and well-drained soil. **Zones 7–10**

Pennisetum glaucum
cattail millet

Annual with broad straplike leaves that form a mound to 48 inches tall and 3 feet across. Cattail-like cones encrusted with deep yellow flowers rise a foot above in late summer and then produce seed that small birds flock to eat. Fast growing and easy from seed. Has been grown throughout history as a protein-rich grain in Africa, Asia, India. 'Purple Majesty' has dark purple-brown foliage and stalks.

Preferences Full sun and well-drained loam. Requires warm soil temperatures to germinate. Not tolerant of drought or wet soil.

Photinia melanocarpa 'Viking'

Photinia melanocarpa
black chokeberry

Rounded shrub native to eastern North America grows 3 to 6 feet tall and broad. Suckers to form dense growth, good habitat for nesting songbirds. White flowers in early summer are followed by black-blue berries that hang on until early spring, offering birds food during a lean time. Berries become more palatable for people after a frost too; astringent, they make strong wine or juice high in antioxidants. Fruit is high in pectin, useful for combining with other fruits for jellies and jams. Dark green glossy foliage turns blazing red in fall, a great substitute for invasive burning bush (*Euonymus alata*). Good in rain gardens.

Preferences Moist, acidic soil. Very flood tolerant. **Zones 3–9**

Prunus ×yedoensis
Yoshino cherry

Medium-sized tree, 30 to 40 feet high and broad, bears stunning masses of white, very fragrant blooms in early spring. Serrated oval leaves to 5 inches long turn showy golden orange in fall. Small, bitter fruits attract birds, and flowers attract butterflies.

Preferences Full sun to light shade. Tolerates humidity and heat but needs regular moisture and good drainage. **Zones 5–8**

Rhus typhina 'Bailtiger'

Rhus typhina
staghorn sumac

Native to eastern North America, the species grows to 20 feet tall and wide, suckering to form extensive thickets. New branches are velvety like a young stag's horns. Pointed panicles of clustered yellow-green flowers in midsummer turn to showy rust-red hairy berries (on female plants) lasting through winter. Brilliant red-orange fall color. Provides food and shelter for more than a hundred bird species. Good on slopes for erosion control, or where spread can be checked by mowing. Berry clusters make a delicious pink "lemonade." Compact form 'Bailtiger' grows slowly with minimal suckering to 4 to 5 feet tall and broad, with bright orange fall color.

Preferences Full sun to light shade. Needs well-drained soil. Tolerates juglone, drought, poor soil, and pollution. **Zones 3–8**

Ribes odoratum
clove currant

Medium-sized deciduous shrub, rounded, grows to 4 to 7 feet tall and broad. Native to central United States. Late spring blooms, yellow with orange eyes, exude a strong aromatic smell of cloves. Juicy, mild-flavored black fruits on female plants can be eaten fresh or in jams, juices, pies. Attracts butterflies, bees, and

birds. Good rain garden plant. Lobed leaves turn dull yellow in fall. Will spread by suckering and self-sowing. 'Crandall' resists white pine blister rust.

Preferences Sun with some afternoon shade, moist to wet soil. Tolerates clay and lime. Protect from strong wind and dry soil. **Zones 4–8**

Rubus calycinoides
creeping bramble

Gently lobed, coarse-textured, round leaves grow alternately along trailing stems to form dense mats. Evergreen in mild winters, with foliage turning crimson. White flowers in early summer, followed by edible golden-orange fruits that taste like raspberries. Leaves make a mild tea. Good for slopes, path sides, and under taller plants. Tolerates moderate foot traffic. Spreads indefinitely but slowly from rooting stems, about 1 foot a year. Check by mowing adjacent paths.

Preferences Deep shade to full sun. Drought tolerant. Needs good drainage. **Zones 6–9**

Rumex acetosa
sorrel

Herbaceous perennial features upright stalks of oblong, bright green leaves to 8 inches long. Can continue producing new growth all winter in milder areas, even under snow; dies down when the ground freezes. Succulent, juicy, sour leaves flavor sandwiches, salads, soups, and stir fries. Contains oxalic acid, poisonous in large quantities, so eat only minimal amounts and avoid altogether if you tend toward arthritis, gout, kidney stones. Attracts browsers. Cut stems to encourage regrowth of foliage.

Preferences Part shade to sun, moist soil. Tolerates acidic soil. Foliage withstands frost. **Zones 3–9**

Sambucus nigra f. *porphyrophylla* 'Eva'

Sambucus nigra
black elderberry

Lacy-leaved large shrub with slender, brittle branches 10 to 15 feet high and wide blooms in early summer with flat, palm-sized heads of tiny white musky-scented flowers that bow the branches to give a more fountaining effect. Flower buds slightly poisonous; fully ripe flowers can be battered and fried to make elderflower fritters that taste like they smell, or made into delicious, medicinal elderflower cordial. Glossy black berries are edible when fully ripe (slightly poisonous before they ripen) and used for jams, pies, and wines. Do not eat flowers or berries raw. Leaves are poisonous. Suckers to form colonies and self-sows readily in optimum conditions. Useful for rain gardens and shorelines. Attracts birds and butterflies. 'Eva' is more compact, 6 to 8 feet tall and wide, with deep purple leaves and lemon-scented pink flowers. Native American elderberry (*Sambucus canadensis*) is similar and said to have tastier fruit.

Preferences Sun to part shade, moist to wet soil. Branches break in heavy winds and snows. Tolerates heavy clay, pollution, alkalinity. **Zones 4–8**

Schisandra chinensis

schisandra, five-flavor berry

Deciduous perennial vine grows to 30 feet at a moderate rate, twining around a support to climb. Fragrant flowers. Requires both a female and a male plant to produce fruit (dioecious). Highly nutritious, semi-sour bright red fruit in grapelike clusters can be eaten fresh or dried. Aromatic young leaves make good stir-fried greens. Will succeed on the north side of a building. Pale yellow fall color.

Preferences Grows in clay to sand, alkaline to acid soil. Prefers good drainage, rich soil, and regular moisture. Dense to light shade.

Zones 4–10

Sorbus aucuparia 'Joseph Rock'

Sorbus aucuparia
mountain ash, rowan

Small to medium deciduous tree has white flowers in early summer followed by showy clusters of orange berries that attract birds. Pinnate leaves turn yellow to red to burgundy in fall. Effective street tree. Berries, bitter when raw, make decent jellies, or steep them in vodka for rowanberry schnapps. A few cultivars have tart but edible berries.

American mountain ash (*Sorbus americana*) is similar. 'Joseph Rock' has golden-orange berries and burgundy fall foliage.

Preferences Full sun. Needs good drainage. Best in cooler climates. Tolerates a wide range of soils, restricted root zone, moderate road salt, and pollution.
Zones 3–6

Viola canadensis
violet

Herbaceous perennial native to North America has heart-shaped leaves and forms mounds 12 to 14 inches high and wide. Lightly fragrant, showy white flowers with purple markings bloom all summer and fall. Flowers and leaves are edible; fruits, seeds, and rhizomes are not.

Can self-sow to form a dense patch. Useful ground layer under trees and shrubs. Tolerates moderate, regular foot traffic and mowing.

Preferences Full sun to nearly full shade. Moist to wet. Prefers good drainage. Tolerates dense shade, juglone.
Zones 3–8

Plants with Four-Season Structure

Pedestrians may feel a brief thrill as they pass between two sidewalk sentries of beaked yucca (*Yucca rostrata* 'Sapphire Skies').

Acer griseum
paperbark maple

Small, upright deciduous tree grows slowly to 30 feet tall and 20 feet wide. Shiny bronze-red exfoliating bark makes it a four-season specimen. Softly blue-green, trifoliate leaves are paler underneath. Red-tinted to entirely red foliage in late fall.

Preferences Part shade to sun, medium to moist soil. Shelter from strong wind. Tolerates clay. Tolerates restricted root zone. **Zones 4–8**

Agonis flexuosa
peppermint willow

Weeping tree grows 20 to 30 feet tall. Evergreen foliage smells like peppermint when crushed. Fragrant white flowers along branches in summer attract pollinators.

Preferences Full sun to light shade. Highly drought tolerant but prefers moist, well-drained soil. Moderate salt tolerance. Tolerates restricted root zone. **Zones 9–11**

Arctostaphylos densiflora 'Howard McMinn'

Caryopteris ×clandonensis 'Worcester Gold'

Arctostaphylos densiflora
vine hill manzanita

Tall shrub to 7 feet tall and wide has four-season appeal with copious fragrant flowers for the pollinators, broadleaf evergreen foliage, showy red bark, and orange-red fruit for the birds. Slow grower. Doesn't self-sow. Endangered, native to California. 'Howard McMinn' may be easiest variety for garden settings.

Preferences Full to partial sun. Requires excellent drainage, prefers a low-water environment. Salt tolerant. Resents root disturbance. Tolerates restricted root zone. **Zones 7–9**

Caryopteris ×clandonensis
bluebeard, blue spirea

Low, round shrub 2 to 3 feet broad and tall features puffy clusters of fragrant blue flowers from summer through fall after many traditional garden flowers have finished. Aromatic foliage. Attracts butterflies, bees, and other beneficial insects. May die to the ground in colder winters. 'Worcester Gold' has lance-shaped golden leaves and prolific bloom.

Preferences Full sun, medium moisture. Needs good drainage. Drought tolerant. **Zones 5–9**

Cornus sanguinea 'Midwinter Fire'

Catalpa speciosa
northern catalpa

Shade tree native to eastern United States reaches 70 to 100 feet tall with large, heart-shaped leaves to 10 inches across. Large, abundant, fragrant white flowers with purple spots in early summer are followed by foot-long beanlike pods that turn from green to brown and stay into winter, splitting to release seeds. Provides rot-resistant wood used for fence posts. Grows rapidly and produces copious litter. Valuable to honey bees. Has naturalized beyond its native range. Host plant for catalpa sphinx moth, whose larvae (catawba worms) are used as bait for fishing; can be temporarily defoliated, then foliage regrows. Smaller but otherwise similar native southern catalpa (*Catalpa bignonioides*), to 25 to 50 feet, may be better for West Coast and Deep South.

Preferences Full sun to part shade. Deep, moist soil (but very adaptable). Tolerates clay soil and seasonal flooding. **Zones 4–8 northern, 5–9 southern**

Cordyline australis
cabbage tree

Tall, narrow, palmlike tree grows to 6 to 15 feet tall. Swordlike evergreen leaves are up to 3 feet long. Showy, fragrant panicles of flowers appear in late spring. Has established naturalized populations in some California forest understories.

Preferences Full sun to part shade, boggy to dry soil. Tolerates restricted root zone. **Zones 9–11**

Cornus sanguinea
bloodtwig dogwood

Deciduous shrub grows to 6 by 6 feet and slowly suckers to form colonies. Fragrant heads of tiny white flowers in early summer attract butterflies. Dark purple summer fruit attracts birds. Good fall leaf color and vivid red stems in winter to early spring. Effective erosion control or rain garden plant. 'Midwinter Fire' has red-tipped yellow stems and golden fall foliage.

Preferences Full sun to part shade. Well-drained, consistently moist soil. **Zones 4–8**

Cotinus coggygria 'Royal Purple'

Cotinus coggygria
European smokebush

Small multitrunked tree or tall shrub with a rounded shape grows to 10 to 15 feet tall and wide. Blue-green oval leaves radiate from stems; fall color ranges from yellow-orange to purple-red. In summer, wispy clouds of pink seed heads catch the sun and give the impression of smoke hovering over the plant. Purple-leaved varieties generally have bolder fall color than the species. Similar American smoketree (*Cotinus obovatus*), native to southern United States, is larger, to 20 to 30 feet tall and wide.

Preferences Full sun to light shade, medium moisture with good to average drainage. Tolerates clay, drought, and restricted root zone. **Zones 4–8**

Crataegus phaenopyrum
Washington hawthorn

Native to southeastern United States, this small tree to 20 to 30 feet high and 20 feet wide has four-season appeal for humans and wildlife. Leaves emerge red tinted, green in summer. Fragrant white blooms in early summer attract butterflies. Showy fall foliage (unlike other hawthorns) is rust red. Red berries from summer through winter provide bird food, attracting cardinals, robins, and blue jays, and thorns make great nesting sites and cover. Sheds thorns, so don't go barefoot under it. Alternate host for cedar-quince rust. For northern ranges, eastern North American native cockspur hawthorn (*Crataegus crus-galli*) is similar but without fall color.

Preferences Sun to light shade, low but regular water. Tolerates compacted soil, drought, heat, air pollution, salt, and restricted root zone. **Zones 3–8**

Deutzia gracilis 'Nikko'

Deutzia gracilis
slender deutzia

Low-growing deciduous shrub reaches to 5 feet high and wide with deep green ovate leaves on gracefully arching stems. Profuse white fragrant blooms are produced in late spring. Stems die periodically; needs some pruning to remove dead growth. 'Nikko' is a compact form to 2 feet high with flowers held more above foliage and deep burgundy fall color.

Preferences Part shade to full sun. Medium moisture. Tolerates clay soil. **Zones 5–8**

Diervilla lonicera
northern bush honeysuckle

Hardy, low, suckering shrub with dense, arching stems spreads slowly to form an easy-care hedge or thicket. Small yellow trumpet-shaped flowers cover the shrub in early summer. Multicolored fall foliage shows pink, orange, and red/bronze tints. Native to north-central and eastern North America. Good rain garden plant. 'Copper' (dwarf bush honeysuckle) is a compact form with red-tinted leaves.

Preferences Tolerates a wide range of soils and light conditions. **Zones 4–8**

Hamamelis ×intermedia 'Arnold Promise'

Edgeworthia chrysantha
oriental paperbush

Rounded deciduous shrub grows to 4 to 5 feet tall and wide. Faintly fragrant, showy, uniquely shaped blooms in very early spring before leaves emerge make a striking show against the dark branches. Dark green deciduous leaves emerge fuzzy. Purple-green berries. Buds interesting over winter.

Preferences Low but regular moisture, good drainage. Tolerates clay. Resents root disturbance. **Zones 7–10**

Hamamelis ×intermedia
witch hazel

Vase-shaped deciduous understory shrub or small tree grows to 12 to 15 feet tall and wide. Ribbonlike flowers bloom along stems in late winter. Oval leaves 3 to 6 inches long have a puckery surface and fall color of yellow to yellow-orange. Shares space well with large trees. 'Arnold Promise' has sweetly fragrant, bright yellow flowers with dark red markings and blooms later than other cultivars. Remove suckers to prevent them overgrowing the cultivar. *Hamamelis vernalis*, native to southern United States, is similar. *Hamamelis virginiana*, native throughout eastern North America, grows larger and looser with less-conspicuous (though quite fragrant) flowers in late autumn.

Preferences Rich, acidic soils with medium moisture and good drainage. Full sun to part shade. **Zones 5–8**

Illicium parviflorum 'Florida Sunshine'

Ilex vomitoria
yaupon holly

Quick-growing small tree native to southeastern United States has tiny, leathery, evergreen leaves and withstands frequent shearing. Female plants produce bright red winter berries that feed migrating birds. Spring nectar source for small butterflies, larval food for hairstreaks and skippers. 'Schilling's Dwarf' grows 6 feet high and wide and does not fruit.

Preferences Any soil moisture, full sun to full shade. Tolerates salt and restricted root zone. **Zones 8–10**

Illicium parviflorum
yellow anise tree

Small, narrow, multitrunked tree or large shrub native to Florida grows to 15 feet tall and half as wide. Shiny evergreen foliage is anise scented. Inconspicuous yellow-green flowers in early summer become showy star-shaped fruit. Spreads by root suckers to form colonies; branches root where they touch the soil. Good rain garden plant, useful near homes where moisture collects. Listed as a threatened species. 'Florida Sunshine' (zones 6–9) has ivory-colored foliage to brighten a shady spot.

Preferences Part to dense shade, consistently moist to wet soil. Tolerates restricted root zone. **Zones 7–10**

Loropetalum chinense 'Ruby'

Loropetalum chinense
Chinese fringe flower

Broadleaf evergreen, medium-sized, rounded shrub reaches 4 to 8 feet tall and wide. Leaves range from green with red to burgundy tints to entirely red. White ribbonlike blooms appear in late winter. 'Ruby' has showy, unscented bright pink flowers; good substitute for invasive Japanese barberry (*Berberis thunbergii*).

Preferences Best in sun with some afternoon shade, in well-drained but consistently moist soil. Needs good drainage and some acidity. Protect from strong winds. **Zones 7–10**

Microbiota decussata
Russian arborvitae, Siberian cypress

Low, feathery, needled evergreen shrub grows 1 to 2 feet high and spreads to 4 to 12 feet wide. Foliage turns gray-purple to bronze in winter. Useful ground cover under pines and other evergreens where some light comes in under the canopy.

Preferences Full sun to part shade. Needs regular moisture and afternoon shade in hotter regions. **Zones 3–7**

Nyssa sylvatica
tupelo, black gum

Slow-growing shade tree native to eastern North America grows to 80 feet tall and half as wide with architectural form and brilliant scarlet fall foliage. Females produce dark fruit, attracting birds. Inconspicuous flowers are great for bees. Try swamp tupelo (*Nyssa sylvatica* var. *biflora*) in wetter southern sites.

Preferences Sun to part shade, best with regular moisture but tolerates both drought and periodic flooding. Prefers somewhat acidic soil. Resents transplanting. Tolerates clay, compacted soil, and restricted root zone. **Zones 5–9**

Parkinsonia aculeata
palo verde

Small, fine-textured, fast-growing, broad-crowned tree native to southern United States reaches 15 to 20 feet tall and 20 to 25 feet wide. Produces fragrant yellow orchidlike flower sprays throughout summer after rains. Seedpods are 3 to 5 inches long and look like flat brown string beans. Small leaves often shed during summer, though green-tinted stems continue to photosynthesize. Thorny, making it a good nesting site for birds. Nectar and pods are food for bees, butterflies, birds, and small mammals. Good honey plant.

Preferences Requires full sun and excellent drainage. Tolerates restricted root zone, drought, heat, and salt. **Zones 8–11**

Paxistima canbyi
cliff green

Tiny-leaved, dense evergreen shrub, 6 to 12 inches high, spreads very slowly to 3 to 4 feet or more. Native to eastern United States. Glossy, needlelike dark green leaves look prickly but are smooth to the touch. Foliage may bronze in winter; may burn in severe cold.

Great ground cover on the sunny side of taller shrubs and beside walkways.

Preferences Full sun to some shade. Moist, well-drained, somewhat rich soil. Tolerates alkaline soil, clay, and salt. **Zones 3–9**

Physocarpus opulifolius
ninebark

Native to central and eastern North America, this arching deciduous shrub grows 6 to 8 feet high and 6 feet wide. Peeling multicolored apricot-brown-white bark is showy in winter, as are prominent black clusters of seed heads arranged in horizontal layers along the branches. In summer, fuzzy flat clustered flower heads contain dark pink buds opening into tiny white flowers. Good rain garden plant. Purple-leaved cultivars are available.

Preferences Full sun to part shade, moist to dry. Drought tolerant once established. Tolerates seasonal flooding, clay, infertility. **Zones 2–8**

Populus tremuloides
quaking aspen

Small to medium-sized tree native throughout North America, fast growing and short lived, forms clonal colonies through suckering and seeding. Ghostly gray to golden trunk, depending on origin, with black markings. Oval, green, powdery leaves with prominent light-colored veins flutter audibly in the slightest breeze. Deep golden yellow fall color. Branches have a sharp, fresh smell year-round. Valuable wildlife habitat, hosting a variety of insects including butterflies.

Preferences Tolerates a variety of soils in cool climates. Prefers moist, well-drained, acidic soil. Protect from heat and afternoon sun. Intolerant of urban pollution.
Zones 1–6

Quercus gambelii
Gambel oak

Large multitrunked shrub native to intermountain and southwestern United States can be trained as a single-trunked small tree that grows slowly to 30 feet tall. Glossy green, leathery leaves have pale underside, fall color brown to dull red. Produces acorns enjoyed by deer, small mammals, and birds (woodpeckers, jays, pigeons). Grows naturally in clonal groves or thickets. *Quercus hypoleucoides* (silverleaf oak), zones 7–10, is similar in habit but evergreen, with long, narrow leaves dark green above and woolly white underneath.

Preferences Well-drained soils. Tolerates restricted root zone and drought. Deep-rooted, resents moving.
Zones 4–7

Thuja occidentalis 'Degroot's Spire'

Thuja occidentalis
eastern white cedar, American arborvitae

Native to eastern North America, this evergreen with flat panels of needles assumes a pyramidal shape, 15 to 20 feet tall and 10 to 15 feet wide. Foliage can brown in winter in exposed or dry locations, then will green again in spring. Slow-growing pillar-shaped 'Degroot's Spire' stays skinny, gradually reaching 15 to 20 feet tall and 4 to 6 feet wide.

Preferences Full sun to part shade, regular moisture. Tolerates clay, pollution, juglone. Prefers alkaline soil. Protect from afternoon sun in southern regions. **Zones 2–7**

Viburnum carlesii
Korean spice viburnum

Medium-sized shrub grows 4 to 6 feet tall and wide. Extremely fragrant 3- to 4-inch heads of white blooms unfurl from dark pink buds in early spring. Blue-black berries in late summer feed the birds. Dark green matte leaves turn dull red to burgundy in fall.

Preferences Part shade to full sun. Tolerates a variety of soils and conditions. Juglone tolerant. **Zones 4–7**

Weigela florida 'Java Red'

Yucca rostrata 'Sapphire Skies'

Viburnum dentatum
arrowwood viburnum

Large, densely branched deciduous shrub, native to eastern United States, reaches 6 to 10 feet tall and spreads slowly by suckers. Showy flat heads of white flowers in early spring and red berries ripening to black in late summer attract birds and small mammals. Glossy, oval, toothed leaves are dark green; fall color varies by plant from yellow to orange to red. Tough, dependable plant for habitat and hedges. Walter's viburnum (*Viburnum obovatum*, zones 6–9), has similar habit and native range.

Preferences Full sun to part shade. Prefers moist soil but drought tolerant once established. Tolerates clay and juglone. **Zones 2–8**

Weigela florida
weigela

Deciduous medium-sized shrub with a fountaining form can grow to 8 to 10 feet tall and wide. In early summer its pink, funnel-shaped flowers attract hummingbirds. Firewise landscape plant. Compact form 'Java Red' usually grows 4 to 5 feet tall and broad, has purple-tinged foliage and red buds that open into pink flowers.

Preferences Full sun to light shade. Regular moisture and good drainage. Tolerates clay. **Zones 4–8**

Yucca rostrata
beaked yucca

Evergreen tree cactus native to Texas and Mexico grows to 6 to 12 feet tall with a trunk 5 to 8 inches in diameter. Stiff, swordlike leaves to 3 feet long form spiny masses at the top. Sturdy 2-to-3-foot flower stalks of creamy white appear above foliage in spring. 'Sapphire Skies' has bluer foliage than the species, and its softer, less rigid leaves make it a better choice near walkways.

Preferences Full sun. Free-draining alkaline soil. Resents water in winter. **Zones 5–11**

Hardiness Zones and Metric Conversions

Plant hardiness zones
Average annual minimum temperature

Zone	Temperature (deg. F)			Temperature (deg. C)		
1	Below		-50	Below		-46
2	-50	to	-40	-46	to	-40
3	-40	to	-30	-40	to	-34
4	-30	to	-20	-34	to	-29
5	-20	to	-10	-29	to	-23
6	-10	to	0	-23	to	-18
7	0	to	10	-18	to	-12
8	10	to	20	-12	to	-7
9	20	to	30	-7	to	-1
10	30	to	40	-1	to	4
11	40	and	above	4	and	above

To see the U.S. Department of Agriculture Hardiness Zone Map,
visit planthardiness.ars.usda.gov/PHZMWeb/.
For Canada, go to planthardiness.gc.ca/
or sis.agr.gc.ca/cansis/nsdb/climate/hardiness/index.html.

Leaving gaps in the foliage
to glimpse the distant hills,
or even the house across the
street, lends depth to a shallow
hellstrip garden.

Conversion tables

inches	centimeters
¼	0.6
½	1.3
1	2.5
2	5.1
3	7.6
4	10
5	13
6	15
7	18
8	20
9	23
10	25

feet	meters
1	0.3
2	0.6
3	0.9
4	1.2
5	1.5
10	3
20	6
30	9
40	12
50	15
60	18
100	30

Suggestions for Further Reading

Bornstein, Carol, David Fross, and Bart O'Brien. 2011. *Reimagining the California Lawn: Water-Conserving Plants, Practices, and Designs*. Los Olivos, CA: Kachuma Press.

Ellis, Barbara. 2007. *Covering Ground: Unexpected Ideas for Landscaping with Colorful, Low-Maintenance Ground Covers*. North Adams, MA: Storey Publishing.

Goodnick, Billy. 2013. *Yards: Turn Any Outdoor Space into the Garden of Your Dreams*. Pittsburgh, PA: St. Lynn's Press.

Hadden, Evelyn J. 2012. *Beautiful No-Mow Yards: 50 Amazing Lawn Alternatives*. Portland, OR: Timber Press.

Kourik, Robert. 2012. *Greater Garden Yields with Drip Irrigation: It's Not Just for Droughts Anymore* (eBook). Occidental, CA: Metamorphic Press.

Lowenfels, Jeff, and Wayne Lewis. 2006. *Teaming with Microbes: A Gardener's Guide to the Soil Food Web*. Portland, OR: Timber Press.

Penick, Pam. 2013. *Lawn Gone! Low-Maintenance, Sustainable, Attractive Alternatives for Your Yard*. Berkeley, CA: Ten Speed Press.

Primeau, Liz. 2010. *Front Yard Gardens: Growing More than Grass* (2nd edition). Ontario, Canada: Firefly Books.

Ogden, Lauren Springer. 2011. *The Undaunted Garden: Planting for Weather-Resilient Beauty* (2nd edition). Golden, CO: Fulcrum Publishing.

Ogden, Scott, and Lauren Springer Ogden. 2011. *Waterwise Plants for Sustainable Gardens: 200 Drought-Tolerant Choices for All Climates*. Portland, OR: Timber Press.

Tallamy, Douglas W. 2009. *Bringing Nature Home: How Native Plants Sustain Wildlife in Our Gardens* (updated and expanded edition). Portland, OR: Timber Press.

Acknowledgments

I want to thank Tom Fischer for approaching me with this topic, and for his calm humor during the process of creating this book. Editors Eve Goodman and Lorraine Anderson have vastly improved it with their gentle but thorough attention. I am grateful for the author-centered culture at Timber Press and feel fortunate to work with them again.

We all benefit from the adventurous spirit of hell-strip pioneer Lauren Springer Ogden, who along with her husband, Scott, continues to develop regionally appropriate plants and designs that inject nature into our busy modern lives. Lauren has been a generous supporter and mentor throughout this project, and in fact I have admired her from afar since reading her book *The Undaunted Garden*; it caught my attention at first glance and helped to guide me through the process of creating my first garden.

Josh McCullough, whose passion and artistry are apparent in his images throughout the book, lent his enthusiasm and support as well, and he has been a pleasure to work with. I am also pleased to include photographs from animal lover Hunter Ten Broeck, volcano lover and sculptor Dan Corson, and Florida-friendly gardener Kurt Vigneau, as well as waterwise landscape architect Kate Stickley. Scott Ogden and Lauren Springer Ogden graciously allowed me to include their photos as well. Thanks to Mary, Bobbi, Lauren, and Daphne for letting me use their likenesses to illustrate important concepts.

The following kind and knowledgeable people read the manuscript and provided detailed feedback that has improved it tremendously, and I thank them for their generous help: Susan Harris, my friend, mentor, and co-conspirator in the Lawn Reform Coalition; my dear sister Sherilyn Orr, brilliant of mind and generous of spirit; Karen Graham, the best brainstorming buddy; Susan Damon, hellstrip gardener extraordinaire; and regional garden gurus Marte Hult, Kelly Marshall, and Lucy Dinsmore. Many other individuals answered my questions, identified plants and animals, and clarified concepts for me, and I appreciate all the help I've received.

It has been a joy to explore the gardens featured herein, to hear each gardener's unique stories and clever strategies, and of course I have loved learning about more new plants, especially those that will not grow in my Minnesota garden. I appreciate these dear people's willingness to open their gardens to me, and now to you as well, and the time they took to explain, refine, verify, and chew the fat throughout the process of getting the words right.

My mother has been my staunch supporter throughout my life, and my husband through the last couple of decades. They have made it possible for me to spend years of my life writing books about gardens, for which I am more grateful than I can ever express.

Photo and Location Credits

Photos

Dan Corson, 66–67 top

Josh McCullough, 2, 6 top, 10, 15, 17 top left and top right, 18–19, 21, 23–33, 39–43, 45, 59–65, 66–67 bottom, 67 right, 73 right, 93 right, 100–109, 112, 114, 125–134, 136 left, 138 left, 144–145 center, 146–147, 152 left, 155, 158–162, 165 left, 168, 171–183, 188–190, 194, 199–200, 204–206, 213, 217, 218, 223 left, 224–225, 225 center, 226 right, 227 right, 228 left and center, 230 center, 234 right, 235 right, 236 left, 236–237 center, 238 left, 238–239 center, 239 center right, 243–244, 245 left, 246, 247 left, 248, 250 right, 252–253 center, 253–254, 255 center and right, 257 left, 258 left, 260–262, 263 left, 264–266, 267 center and right, 268, 270 right, 271 right, 272–273, 275 left, 276 right, 277–278

Lauren Springer Ogden, 13, 22 bottom, 51 top, 219, 224 center, 227 left, 229 center left

Scott Ogden, 48, 142

Kate Stickley, 44

Hunter Ten Broeck, 150, 152 right

Kurt Vigneau, 88–91, 92–93 center, 216, 259 right

All other photos are by Evelyn J. Hadden.

Locations / Designers / Artists

Arterra Landscape Architects, San Francisco, California, 40–43, 234 right, 254 left, 265 right

The Bakken Museum, Minneapolis, Minnesota, 225 right

Jeffrey Bale pebble mosaic, 171

Jesse Benson garden, Minneapolis, Minnesota, 34–38, 230–231 center, 255 left

Bobbi and Tim Carlin garden, Boulder, Colorado, design by Lauren Springer Ogden and Scott Ogden, 46, 49–52, 53 left, 195, 226 left, 229 left center, 234 left center, 235 left, 239 right, 240 left

Chanticleer, Wayne, Pennsylvania, 192, 270 left

Ted Chapman garden, Newton Lower Falls, Massachusetts, design by Ted Chapman, landscape designer, 39, 182, 235 right, 262

Rebecca Chesin garden, Plymouth, Minnesota, 187 right, 229 left

Dan Corson and Berndt Stugger garden, Seattle, Washington, 23, 60–65, 66–67 center, 245 left, 267 right, 270 right

Jessica Cortright and Hans Germann garden, Boise, Idaho, 80–86, 87 left, 238 center, 257 right

Cottonwood Grille, Boise, Idaho, design by The Land Group and RMH Company, 186

Laura Crockett garden, Portland, Oregon, design by Laura Crockett, GardenDiva, 21 right, 26–32, 180–181, 190, 218, 236 left, 247 left

Susan and Paul Damon garden, Saint Paul, Minnesota, 136 right, 229 right

Daniel Stowe Botanical Garden, Belmont, North Carolina, 232–233, 241 right, 256 left

Darcy Daniels garden, Portland, Oregon, design by Darcy Daniels, Bloomtown Gardens, 188–189

Index

MITCH KEZAR

About the Author

Speaker and author Evelyn Hadden encourages property owners to convert unused, unloved lawns to more rewarding landscapes. An avid pedestrian, she applauds the generosity behind curbside gardens and the growing push to remake front yards, hellstrips, parking lots, and medians with appealing and useful gardens.

Her book *Beautiful No-Mow Yards* has been a Timber Press best seller since it was published in 2012. Her garden memoir *Apprentice to a Garden* won two gold medals, and *Shrink Your Lawn*, a photo-rich take-home for audiences of her talks, won a silver.

Evelyn founded the informational website LessLawn.com and is a founding member of the national Lawn Reform Coalition, a resource for earth-friendly lawn care and lawn alternatives, as well as a partner in the provocative team blog Garden Rant.

Find out more about her at EvelynHadden.com.